ELEANOR GARVIN

AT HOME
in
BURGUNDY
—
THE
PAPILLON RECIPES

ELEANOR GARVIN

D0939913

**WINE NOTES AND PHOTOS
BY DENNIS SHERMAN**

www.eldenwine.com
foodstuff.eldenwine.com
www.papillonselect.com

ISBN: 1-4392-3981-9
ISBN-13: 9781439239810

Visit www.booksurge.com to order additional copies.

TABLE OF CONTENTS

PREFACE

Papillon Select Tours was a natural development from our many years at the helm of the hotel barge, Le Papillon. In 1992 we decided to take the concept of a barge holiday--hosting small private parties on the waterways of France--on to dry land. No longer was Ellie constrained by a tight galley or Dennis' selected wines by the hold under the floor. Best of all we were no longer limited to the network of canals, we could run our weeks wherever we found a suitable house. For sixteen years we have hosted small house parties in some of the most beautiful and interesting regions of France, Italy and Spain: Tuscany, Umbria, Sicily, Burgundy, Provence, the Basque Country.

This formula was an immediate success. Papillon has become almost a club as our parties faithfully follow us around the Mediterranean tasting the delights of each region. After a morning in the market with Ellie, an instructive walk through the vineyards with Dennis or a historical tour with me, what could be better than to return to the house, to a beautifully situated terrace and Ellie's renowned buffet lunch, all to be enjoyed in the company of chosen friends?

Spending time in each region has allowed us to search out the choicest of ingredients, build relationships with the locals and understand the culinary traditions of each location. Cooking in large country kitchens for small appreciative parties has enabled Ellie to offer exceptional menus each day. Her delicate touch, understanding of ingredients and eye for colour and presentation have won her the admiration of our guests. This wonderful cookbook has been compiled in answer to their many requests.

Jamie Blair Gould

Photo: Gilles Crampes/ Paris

INTRODUCTION

This is a personal story. It is a collection of recipes that I have cooked for clients and friends during the 25 years that my husband, Dennis, and I have lived in France. It also tells of how we made our home in Burgundy.

What began as a summer adventure when I was 23 turned into a new life in a new world. Dennis and I set out from Annapolis, Maryland in 1983 with a couple of one-way tickets to Europe and the money from the sale of my car. We were going to apprentice ourselves to the great chefs of France. I met Dennis while we were working in the kitchen of 'Les Survivants'. (He always says we *consommé-d* our relationship). Claire Owens, the owner-chef had cooked in Paris; and for that, 'Les Survivants' was ahead of its time. Claire said that if we were really serious about food we should go to France. So we did.

After a summer-long series of adventures and missteps, we arrived in Avignon in September. Money was low; the great chefs were not forthcoming. So we went for a temporary fix. The grape harvest was beginning, and Chateau St. Roch near Roquemaure was hiring. We pitched a tent under the pines in the winemaker's back garden, and became part of a mixed crew of locals and migrant workers. The picking lasted five weeks, and that first day an eternity. We didn't have the muscles, but we were too proud not to keep the pace. Work started brightly in the cool morning mist, but the Provençal sun was soon overhead. We broke for lunch and collapsed. By the end of the afternoon, the knees gave out, and we literally crawled to the end of the last row. Then, back at the tent, exhausted, it dawned on us that we had nothing to eat.

Camping, our cooking facilities were limited. Though not as limited as our language skills. We set off to the shops with a dictionary, the present tense and a shaky grasp of whole numbers. Standing in front of the *charcuterie*, we realized that we knew the word 'kilo', but not the word for 'half' and other useful shopping terms. So we ordered a kilo of pâté, a kilo of Roquefort cheese and a kilo of something called *gras double*. That, a *baguette* and a liter of Cotes du Rhone, and we were set. Dinner back at the tent was a triumph; we had arrived and survived. The pâté and the Roquefort were great—a month's supply, but very good. The big slices of *gras double* were just weird. (We learned a few weeks later that this is tripe in jelly, and it's meant to be stewed.) Luckily—well, at least for us—we returned to our camp the following lunchtime to find the winemaker's dog writhing outside our tent. He had knocked over our cooler and eaten the whole lot, not far from seven pounds of the stuff dreams are made of!

These weeks in Roquemaure set in motion a series of coincidences that changed our lives. One of the cellar workers, a young wine maker from Cognac who was there for work experience, had traveled in the US, and was sympathetic to our story. He was soon as determined as we were that we should cook in France. So while we were out picking grapes, our new friend was writing letters and making phone calls.

The harvest ended. We took an apartment in town, trading cooking and housekeeping for rent. Winter came. We found jobs in a *creperie* near the market hall in Avignon. At least we were cooking. In the Spring, persistence paid off. A job offer. It was the Bombard Society; they had received our *résumé* from Steven Spurrier at the *Ecole du Vin* in Paris who got it from our friend in Roquemaure. The Bombard Society, they said, organizes hot-air balloon trips in Burgundy; and they were looking for a *chef du picnic*. It was a job for one person, but they had no objection to us sharing it. And the salary seemed like a fortune to us at the time.

So in April, we said good-bye to Avignon and headed north to Burgundy. The Bombard people met us off the train in Beaune and took us to their base, the gate house and *orangerie* of what had once been a magnificent chateau. Our kitchen was round, one of the ruined-chateau towers. The season was about to begin. Balloon pilots and crew were arriving daily. We were to cook while the operation was being fitted out, so we went shopping immediately and stayed up most of that first night, prepping stocks, making pastry, and organizing our kitchen. It was a night to remember.

Buddy Bombard's Great Balloon Adventure is just that. Buddy is a pioneer of the sport. He proposes a week of ballooning and fine food. Flights take place either early in the morning or in the late afternoon when the winds die. So lunch is the main meal of the day, invariably a Michelin-rated affair. Our job was to provide an elegant buffet in the evening. We called it 'meals on wheels' because we brought everything: tables and chairs; plates and glasses; tablecloths, cutlery, flowers and candles. And every evening we laid a spread and set the mood in the great hall of some chateau, to await the arrival of the balloonists.

We passed the Spring in Burgundy, shuttling between Beaune and the Mor-van, where our lunchtime competition was the rising star Bernard Loiseau in Saulieu. We moved to Bombard's Loire Valley base in mid-summer, and set up our buffets in some of the most magnificent chateaux and gardens on earth. The food may have been cold, but we were hot. Finally we had our fingers in real French cuisine.

We left Bombard at the end of the season with plans to spend the winter in sunny Spain. But we'd not yet seen Paris. So before heading south, we spent a month walking the streets of the most beautiful city in the world. We found a centrally-located, very cheap hotel (where we had to take the door off the armoire and put it under the mattress for support), and jumped headlong into a few weeks of culinary indulgence. The best of French regional cuisine can be found in Paris. It's all there, micro-cosmopolitan. We walked for miles, work-ing up an appetite, talking about food and what to eat next. It didn't have to be fancy; it just had to be French.

By December, we were on a balcony above the beach north of Alicante. We spent the winter grilling sardines, diving for sea urchins and lazing over paella at Coco's beach shack. The Alicante market is a hall of marble slabs piled high with dead-fresh fish. We had Alan Davidson's 'Mediterranean Seafood' with us; and there it all was, laid out before us. This was the Med; we had it all. We would watch from our apartment as scuba divers leapt off the rocks with spear guns, to emerge minutes later with a skewered catch. I can still see one little man--he looked like Gandhi--who would wade into a cove with a trident and a tiny sack of pebbles tied to a string. He'd wiggle the sack among the rocks, an octopus would attack, and he'd spear it. Taking hold of it by the tentacles, he went to the rocks and beat it to a pulp. To tenderize it, we assumed. Who needs TV?

By March we were nearly broke again. Kids! Via Bombard, we received a call from a hotel-barge company looking for crew in Alsace. The boat was called *Panache*, and she had just been refitted to carry eight passengers. For this, her first season, she would ply the *Canal de la Marne au Rhine* between Strasbourg and Nancy. The owner-captain, Guy Bardet, is what the French call a *fine bouche*, a discerning palate. He would market *Panache* as a food and wine cruise. So we had to prove ourselves again, this time to a Frenchman.

Alsatian food is often characterized as glorified sauerkraut and sausage. But nothing could be further from the truth; it is among the most varied and refined of any regional cuisine in France. So there we were, in an entirely new and different region, with an essentially unlimited budget and a captive audience of enthusiastic guests expecting to see something exciting at each meal. What more could we ask for? It was an amazing season, and we were sad to sail out of Alsace at the year's end. But home port for *Panache* was Burgundy, so we were going back. Little did we know for how long!

We were pleased when Guy asked us to take on one of the fleet's larger boats the following year. *Litote* is a 20 passenger barge with a crew of 8. Cruising the Burgundy canal, Dijon was our home port. It was 1986, our third year in France; and we knew then that we wanted to stay. We had not found that dream apprenticeship, but we had fallen into something much more interesting. Here we were, cruising from market town to market town, living and breathing French cuisine. It was like having our own restaurant, except that we hadn't had to sell our souls.

It was there on *Litote* that we met Bill Higgs. Bill grew up on the English canals, a natural born captain. With him at the helm, we hatched the idea of buying a boat and running our own show. And it just so happened that a sweet little antique barge was on the market. We set sail with *Le Papillon* in the Spring of 1988. She would be our home for the next decade. We catered to groups of six, usually three couples traveling together. It was like hosting a week-long dinner party. There was a spirit of adventure. Soon we had a loyal following, which meant that we had to change our itinerary regularly. So over the years, we cruised the length and breadth of France, and I learned French cuisine in a way that I could never have imagined. Dennis, in the meantime, was filling his 'wine bilge' with bottles that our guests could never find at home.

We rented a lock house on the Burgundy Canal, out in the middle of no place. While we didn't work the lock ourselves (lock-keepers accompany boats as they cruise through), we did become part of a community of canal folk who live in a parallel world to those who travel by road. We lived a quarter mile from our nearest neighbors in a splendid green valley. Beside the house was a turning basin, our own private lake, where we moored *Le Papillon* when we were not cruising. We planted a vegetable garden, put up a swing, and without realizing it, put down roots. We shared that house with Bill for a while, until he met Jen.

We often say that Bill showed great foresight in marrying a good cook. All he needed to do then was teach Dennis how to pilot the boat, and *voilà*: we had two independent crews. Bill and Jen worked half the season, and Dennis and I did the other. Enter Jamie. Jamie Blair Gould and Bill grew up together in England. When we bought *Le Papillon,* Jamie offered to do the marketing. It was he who saw the obvious spin-off of our split seasons with Bill and Jen. Our loyal clients were starting to ask where else we could go with the boat. 'Tuscany?' one woman suggested. Dennis and I thought, 'sure, all we need to do is dig a canal!' But lateral-thinking Jamie thought 'villas'.

So with Papillon Select Tours, we took our show onto dry land. Our horizons now reach to wherever we find great cuisine and a good view. We've been across Provence and the Luberon, through the Basque country and into northern Spain. My roots are in Italy, so I have a particular fondness for the diversity that we find ranging through Tuscany and Umbria, Sicily and the northern Lakes. It's true; over the years we've traveled and worked in some of the most beautiful parts of Europe. But though we have often been tempted by Tuscan hills or Basque coastline, every time we come back and see our green, clean, rolling Burgundy, we know we're home.

* * *

BURGUNDY WINE

When we left the United States in 1983, I was your typical American wine enthusiast. Having worked in the wine trade in England for a couple of years in the late 70s, I thought I knew a bit about Bordeaux. And back in Annapolis, we had Mills wine shop where I would spend hours ogling labels from around the world and watching an American wine culture coming to be. Through it all, Burgundy was a mystery. It was expensive. It was complicated. The names were unpronounceable. And if ever you did get a taste, no two wines were ever the same.

So we arrived in Burgundy knowing not much: We knew it's Pinot Noir and Chardonnay; and everybody said Romanée-Conti is the best. But that was about it.

Funny thing though, here the wine wasn't necessarily expensive. Nor was it all that complicated once we saw a map. We learned to pronounce the names, and met a few winemakers. But most importantly, we soon saw that it's just true: no two wines ever do taste the same. In fact, that's the whole point.

In Burgundy, most wines are named after the village they come from. It's the land that's rated, not the winemaker. So you can have a good Pommard or a bad Pommard, depending on who made it. This means that if you want to find good wine, you need to get to know the winemakers. Good winemakers make good wine, whether it's a generic Bourgogne or a lofty Grand Cru.

The problem is that there are thousands of winemakers in Burgundy. And not all of them are good. So where do you start? Well, the best winemakers are farmers first. They are of the earth, and their vines yield beautiful fruit. Without good fruit there is no good wine. We started by asking the locals who they knew who made good wine, and when we found someone whose wines we liked, we would ask them who they knew. Soon we had a clutch of great producers. Not necessarily the most famous ones, but real.

Many of these winemakers produce such small quantities that they never consider the export market. Too much hassle. So when we started buying wine for our hotel-barge *Le Papillon* I was able to serve our guests wines that they could not find back home. In addition, we would visit these wineries as we cruised through the region, and our guests could meet the people who made the wines they were drinking on board.

This was great for everybody. Small-production winemakers treat their wines as they would their children. For them, your enthusiasm is more important than your checkbook; they love to meet the person who will drink their wine. For us, it was an opportunity to develop real relationships with these growers. And visiting them on a regular basis, we got a profound education in Burgundy wine, glass in hand. And for our guests, well, human nature being what it is, we eventually found a way to get these wines back to them. Elden Wine was born of a passion that many of our guests had never experienced. We showed them a true wine culture, something very different to what they knew in the US. For many, it changed the way they look at wine.

It certainly changed ours. It's ironic that Burgundy, whose wines are considered among the rarest and most expensive, should show us such simplicity and humility. We live among farmers. There are of course those here who think themselves 'world class', and often their wines are indeed great. But wine is wine. And Burgundy is a place where the simplest wine can be great too.

> Our website www.eldenwine.com is a chronicle of our education in Burgundy wine. There you will find my newsletters going back to 1996, as well as profiles of many of our favorite winemakers.
>
> Dennis Sherman

BURGUNDIAN SPECIALTIES

BRESSE CHICKENS

Bresse chickens are considered one of the glories of Burgundian cuisine. They carry the 'appellation d'origine controlée' since 1957, and were the first live-stock to be awarded this protection. They are raised according to strict regulations that are based on traditional methods. The breed is unmistakable: red comb, pure white body and blue feet—the French national colors. They are prized for their delicate flavor and the firmness of their flesh. Bresse chickens must come from the region around Bourg-en-Bresse in the Maconnais. They are raised in total liberty, no more than 500 at a time, on grassy fields of at least 15000 square feet (compared to industrial chicken houses where 25–30 birds will share a square yard). They are fed entirely on corn, wheat and dairy products during the 4 months that they are kept (industrial birds are slaughtered at the age of one month). Needless to say, they are not cheap. But they are the real thing.

CASSIS

The black currant grows best in soil apt for vines. This goes a long way to explaining why cassis is so emblematic of Burgundy. But it's only part of the story. When phylloxera destroyed the vineyards of Burgundy at the end of the 19th century, cassis was planted extensively, and the liquor made from the maceration of the black currant berries in alcohol temporarily replaced wine in the region's cafes and bars. And then when the Chanoine Kir, mayor of Dijon in the 1950s, introduced his eponymous cocktail of white Aligote wine with a dash of cassis as the 'vin d'honneur' at official receptions, it became the 'official' fruit of Burgundy.

I have some fantastically productive black currant shrubs in my garden, and at harvest time, I fill my freezer with berries that evoke summer when we use them in the middle of a Burgundian winter. It's one of my favorite flavors. There is no better sorbet.

EPOISSES

Chauvinism is a French word. So you'll forgive me if I say again and again that my favorite cheese comes from the next village over from ours. Epoisses, the village and the cheese, has been a part of our lives as long as we have been in Burgundy. And thanks to the local production by the Fromagerie Berthaut, it can now be part of yours. The Berthaut people have done a fantastic job, perfecting a version of Epoisses that travels well enough to be sold as far away as the US.

Epoisses is a cow's milk cheese in the form of a flat cylinder. Traditionally it was aged on mats made of rye stalks, and dried in the north-east wind. It would be washed regularly with a salt water solution to keep it from developing a crust until the final aging stage where it was washed with *marc de Bourgogne* (a sort of Burgundian grappa). All this took about six weeks. The cheese was then wrapped in a vine leaf and packed in a round wooden box. Things are not so different today. The Berthaut production is no longer open air, and the vine leaf has been replaced with a leaf-shaped paper. But the style of traditional Epoisses has been fairly well preserved.

There are several variations of Epoisses, most notably a cheese also made by the Berthaut folks, known as Aisy Cendré. It's essentially the same cheese, but instead of the *marc* wash, it is dusted with ashes (traditionally from burnt vine cuttings). You might also see a version of Epoisses, another commercial success, called Ami de Chambertin, which is produced not far from Gevrey-Chambertin.

CHEESES (OTHER THAN EPOISSES!)

You'll not be surprised to know that there are other Burgundian cheeses than Epoisses.

Another of my favorites is produced at the abbey of Citeaux, across the valley from Nuits-Saint-Georges. It's a cow's milk cheese, with a washed crust shaped in a large flat disk. It's essentially the same cheese as the Reblochon produced in the Savoie, but the aging period is shorter and the result is a creamy texture and a true taste of the milk. The monks at Citeaux raise their cows on organic pastures. One of the defining qualities of their cheese is its purity.

Another cheese still made to this day by monks comes from the abbey Pierre-Qui-Vire near Vezelay. It is made in a similar way to Citeaux, though smaller and often presented fresher than a Citeaux would be. It is also naturally a bit more pungent.

The Auxerrois produces a cheese that is coming to be better-known outside of Burgundy (thanks again to the Berthaut production in Epoisses). Soumain-train is a cow's milk cheese, with a soft, yellow-orange color. It is aged over several weeks, and is meant to be 'strong'. You'll sometimes see it called Saint Florentin, the name of one of the big co-operatives that produces it. Saint Florentin can also be found fresh, before the aging process, unsalted, and eaten with a sprinkling of sugar.

Down south in the Maconnais, it's goat country, and the most famous of the Burgundian goat cheeses is confusingly named 'Charolais'. Charolais is the name of the region of production. But the same region also gave its name to the famous breed of white cattle that are seen everywhere in Burgundy. So, many think that Charolais must be a cow's milk cheese. To make things worse, sometimes it is—partly. A version is made that's 50-50 cow and goat.

FOIE GRAS

Foie Gras is, of course, the fattened liver of duck or goose (here, it's duck). *'Mi-cuit'* (as opposed to *'Cru'* or 'raw') means it has been prepared and is ready to eat. In this form, it can be easily sliced with a hot knife. *'Entier'* is the best quality. It means that the 'foie gras' is made from one piece of a whole liver. Otherwise, you will find *'bloc'*, which is made from inferior quality livers which are pureed and re-formed. Below that on the scale of quality is *'paté'* which is only partially *foie gras*, usually mixed with pork meat.

Foie gras gets a lot of bad press. But it's actually quite nutritious. It's not nearly as caloric as you might think. 40 grams is 180 kcal. It's a mono-unsaturated fat (like nuts and avocado), and a good source of iron (three times that of beef, but you eat less, of course). It's very rich in Vitamin A and concentrated in B9 and selenium.

JERUSALEM ARTICHOKES

Jerusalem artichokes are not particularly Burgundian, neither are they from Jerusalem, nor are they artichokes. They are the root of a type of sunflower (*girasole* in Italian, 'turn with the sun', which sounds like 'Jerusalem', I guess) that tastes a bit like an artichoke heart. If you want to plant them in the garden, simply take a good specimen from what you buy on the market (avoid knobby ones: they will only produce knobby ones). They grow like a weed, don't give much of a flower; but in the autumn and winter will reward your tolerance with all the roots you care to clear and eat.

MUSTARD

No product is as closely associated with Dijon as mustard. In Burgundy, it replaces butter as a condiment on the table. And it's a main ingredient in many regional recipes. Dijon mustard is a simple concoction—basically mustard seeds and a pungent liquid whirred more or less to a paste. But there are as many styles as there are producers, and as many flavorings as you care to imagine.

Coarser styles are made with white wine vinegar; finer versions use just white wine. One interesting variety (and some say the 'original') uses *verjus*, literally the 'green juice' squeezed from under-ripe grapes. Beyond that it comes down to flavoring: green peppercorn, tarragon, cassis, spice bread, even sweet red pepper. Texture matters, too; *'a l'ancienne'* is coarse, leaving the cracked seeds un-sieved. But by far the most popular is the mild smooth version made famous by the house of Messieurs Grey and Poupon—you know, the one that's commonly found in limousines! These days, Maille makes excellent mustards that are available worldwide. Amora mustards aren't bad either.

But if you want the real thing, one of the last artisanal mustards, look for the name Fallot, and the appellation *moutarde de bourgogne*. Based in Beaune, the Fallot house has taken Burgundian mustard production back to basics, growing their own mustard crop, stone grinding the seeds, using proper Burgundy wines, mostly Aligoté, to make the paste. The result is a pungent, earthy mustard noticeably different from even the best commercial brands. Fallot call it 'Burgundy mustard', and someday it may replace 'Dijon mustard' as the generic name.

RABBIT

We distinguish between not only domesticated and wild rabbits, but also between rabbit and hare. Domesticated rabbit is mild, with delicately flavored, tender flesh. Hare is another animal altogether: larger, with longer legs and bigger ears. Whereas domesticated rabbit can be treated much like chicken, wild rabbit and hare are rich and gamey, and benefit from a marinade and long stewing.

The rabbit loin is the equivalent of the chicken breast. It's the white meat, and tends to cook more quickly, and dry out more easily. It's for this that I suggest using only hind legs if you can find them. On the other hand if you can find just the loins, treat them as you might chicken breast, sautéing or braising them

SNAILS

Be careful when purchasing snails. There are really only two species worth looking for: the Burgundy snail (called *helix pomatia*) and the *petit gris* from Provence (called *helix aspersa*). These taxonomical names should be clearly marked on the label. Almost anything else is likely to be an Asian slug, and not a snail at all. Look for medium- ('*moyen*') or small- ('*petit*') sized snails for these recipes.

The Aperitif

HORS-D'OEUVRES
NIBBLES

FROMAGE DE CHEVRE FRAIS AUX DEUX FIGUES
Canapés of Goat's Cheese with Two Figs

TARTINES DE TAPENADE ET FROMAGE DE CHEVRE A LA TOMATE ROTIE
Goat's Cheese Toasts with Tapenade and Roasted Tomatoes

CANAPÉS DE PAIN D'ÉPICES AUX RILLETTES DE CANARD FUMÉ
Spice Bread with Smoked Duck Rillettes

CREVETTES A L'AVOCAT AUX BAIES ROSES
Shrimp and Avocado with Red Peppercorns

OEUFS DE CAILLE AUX ANCHOIS ET PIMENT D'ESPELETTE
Quail Eggs with Anchovies and Espelette Pepper

ENDIVES AU ROQUEFORT, POMMES ET NOIX
Belgian Endive with Roquefort, Apple and Walnut

PRUNEAUX FARCIS DE CHEVRE AU JAMBON CRU
Prunes Stuffed with Goat's Cheese Wrapped in Cured Ham

CHOUX AU MAQUEREAU FUMÉ ET AU FROMAGE DE CHEVRE
Smoked Mackerel and Goat Cheese Choux Puff

CANAPÉS DE CREVETTES AU CERFEUIL
Shrimp and Chervil Canapés

CANAPÉS DE JAMBON CRU A LA POMME VERTE
Cured Ham and Apple Canapés

GOUGERES
Burgundian Cheese Puffs

COMTÉ MARINÉ AUX ECHALOTES ET AUX HERBES
Marinated Comté Cheese with Shallots and Herbs

CANAPÉS DE FOIE GRAS AU CASSIS ET A L'ANETH
Foie Gras with Cassis and Dill

TARTINES D'OIGNON CONFIT AUX ANCHOIS MARINÉS
Canapés of Slow Cooked Onion and Marinated Anchovy

FROMAGE DE CHEVRE FRAIS AUX DEUX FIGUES
Canapés of Goat's Cheese with Two Figs
20 Pieces

I like to use small, firm, but ripe green figs (as opposed to black figs) for this appetizer.

½ of a vanilla bean
4 tablespoons extra virgin olive oil
¾ cup fresh creamy goat's cheese
4 dried figs minced

2 tablespoons minced fresh chives
Fine sea salt
Freshly ground black pepper
10 small fresh green figs

Split the vanilla bean in half and scrape out the seeds with a knife. Put the seeds in a small bowl and combine with the olive oil.

Mix the goat's cheese with the minced dried figs and chives and season to taste with salt and pepper. Stir in half the vanilla-flavored olive oil.

Slice the fresh figs in half lengthwise. Cut a very thin slice off of the side of each half so that the fig halves will sit flat on a serving plate. Top each half with a teaspoon of goat's cheese, drizzle over the reserved vanilla-flavored oil, season with sea salt and garnish each piece with a sprig of chive. Serve chilled.

TARTINES DE TAPENADE ET FROMAGE DE CHEVRE A LA TOMATE ROTIE

Goat's Cheese Toasts with Tapenade and Roasted Tomatoes
12 *tartines*

Tartines are the French equivalent of Italian *crostini*. Use a crusty sourdough *baguette* split lengthwise to make this *hors-d'oeuvres*.

Keep a jar of quality *tapenade* in the pantry for times when you can't make your own.

3 cups mixed ripe red and yellow cherry tomatoes
3 shallots thinly sliced
Extra virgin olive oil
2 tablespoon fresh thyme leaves
Fine sea salt
Freshly ground black pepper

For the tapenade:
6 anchovy filets soaked in milk for 30 minutes to remove excess salt, then patted dry

2 cups good-quality green olives, pitted
1 tablespoon capers, soaked if salted, or drained if in brine
1 garlic clove minced
1 teaspoon Dijon mustard
6 tablespoons extra virgin olive oil

1 cup fresh creamy goat's cheese or crumbled *crottin*-type goat's cheese.

1 sourdough *baguette* split lengthwise

Make the *tapenade* by combining the anchovies, olives, capers, garlic and mustard in the bowl of a food processor. Process this mixture, stopping the machine occasionally to scrape down the sides with a spatula. When fairly smooth, add the olive oil slowly, drizzling it in as you would when making a mayonnaise. When all four tablespoons have been absorbed, add freshly ground pepper to taste, and then a bit more olive oil if you like.

Preheat the oven to 275°F.

Wash the cherry tomatoes, cut them in half and put them on a piece of parchment paper in one layer on a baking tray. Sprinkle over the shallot slices, drizzle with the olive oil, and season with the salt, pepper and thyme. Bake in a low oven for an hour to concentrate their flavor and sweetness. Remove and reserve.

Increase the oven temperature to 375°F. On each *baguette* half spread a thin layer of the *tapenade*. Top with a layer of goat's cheese and top that with the cherry tomatoes. Put on a baking tray in the hot oven until bubbly, 5 minutes or so. Serve warm.

13

CANAPÉS DE PAIN D'ÉPICES AUX RILLETTES DE CANARD FUMÉ
Spice Bread with Smoked Duck Rillettes
Makes 24 Canapés

There is a spice bread from Dijon that's known throughout France. It is flavored with honey, anise, cinnamon and clove, and can vary from sugar-glazed to 'nature'. You will find a recipe for it in the dessert section. I like it moist and spicy, and often use it in savory recipes. Cubed and turned into croutons, it adds a complex flavor to pumpkin soup. Toasted and turned into fine bread crumbs, it makes a curious crust on sautéed slices of raw *foie gras*, and in the recipe below it complements the smokiness of the duck breast.

6 thin slices *pain d'épices*
I whole smoked duck breast thinly sliced
(try to get at least 30 slices)
4 shallots minced

½ cup red wine
2 tablespoons unsalted butter softened
Minced chive and cracked black pepper to garnish

Reserve 12 slices of the duck breast for garnishing the tops of the canapés. Coarsely chop the remaining duck breast.

Put the minced shallots in a small saucepan with the wine and reduce over low heat to a syrup.

Put the shallots in a food processor with the chopped duck breast. Pulse until fine. Add the softened butter. Remove the crust from the spice bread and quarter each slice. Top each piece with a small knob of the duck rillettes. Gently warm the remaining slices of duck breast in a non-stick pan. Cut each slice in half and top the canapés. Sprinkle with black pepper and chive. Serve warm.

CREVETTES A L'AVOCAT AUX BAIES ROSES
Shrimp and Avocado with Red Peppercorns
Makes 24 hors-d'oeuvres

Served on water biscuits, toast rounds or unflavored tortilla chips, this avocado cream is surprisingly fresh with the addition of diced green apple.

1 teaspoon sherry vinegar
Fine sea salt
2 tablespoons extra virgin olive oil
2 tablespoons heavy cream
1 small shallot minced
½ Granny Smith apple unpeeled and minced

1 ripe avocado minced
24 medium sized cooked shrimp peeled and de-veined
1 tablespoon of slightly crushed red peppercorns
Fresh dill, chives or chervil for garnish

In a small bowl dissolve ½ teaspoon of sea salt in the sherry vinegar. Add the olive oil and cream and whisk to thicken slightly. Add the minced shallot, apple and avocado. Mix well. Keep chilled in the refrigerator until you are ready to make and serve the *hors-d'œuvre*.

Put a teaspoonful of avocado cream on each cracker. Top each with a shrimp and sprinkle over the red peppercorns and fresh dill.

OEUFS DE CAILLE AUX ANCHOIS ET PIMENT D'ESPELETTE
Quail Eggs with Anchovies and Espelette Pepper
10 Servings

These are practical pop-in-your-mouth hors-d'oeuvres. The devil in these eggs comes from the piquancy of the Espelette pepper, a unique flavor from the French Basque region.

20 fresh quail eggs
¼ cup mayonnaise
Pinch of Espelette pepper

10 anchovy filets packed in oil
Fine sea salt
20 large flat parsley leaves

Put the quail eggs in a saucepan and cover with cold water. Bring to a boil for 2 minutes. Drain and shell while still warm.

Split the eggs in half and remove the yolks. Mash the yolks with the mayonnaise, season with Espelette pepper and sea salt to taste. Cut the anchovy filets in half. Refill each egg half with some of the mayonnaise. Top half of the eggs with a piece of anchovy and a parsley leaf. Reform the eggs and skewer with a toothpick. Sprinkle over with Espelette pepper and serve the eggs chilled.

ENDIVES AU ROQUEFORT, POMMES ET NOIX
Belgian Endive with Roquefort, Apple and Walnut
Make 18 spears

4 stalks Belgian endive
¼ cup walnuts coarsely chopped
¼ cup of crumbled Roquefort cheese
1 Granny Smith apple, peeled, cored, minced
1 teaspoon fine sea salt
2 teaspoons sherry vinegar

1 teaspoon Dijon mustard
2 teaspoons fresh chives or dill chopped
1 tablespoon walnut oil
1 teaspoon grated horseradish
4 tablespoons *crème fraîche* or heavy cream

Clean the endive with a damp cloth. Separate 18 of the outer leaves. Slice the endive tips into uniform 2-inch lengths; arrange them on a serving plate

Very thinly, slice the remaining endive and reserve in a salad bowl. Add the walnuts, Roquefort and the minced apple.

In another bowl make the vinaigrette: Dissolve 1 teaspoon of sea salt in the sherry vinegar. Add the mustard, chives, walnut oil, horseradish, and *crème fraîche*. Whisk just to emulsify and toss with the salad. Put a teaspoon of the salad on each spear and serve.

PRUNEAUX FARCIS DE CHEVRE AU JAMBON CRU
Prunes Stuffed with Goat's Cheese Wrapped in Cured Ham
18 hors-d'œuvre

Quick to prepare; easy to serve; a moist, rich hors-d'oeuvre. It takes a little extra time to stuff the prunes but the creaminess of the goat's cheese addition is worth it. Look for good quality pitted extra large prunes to make your life easier.

18 extra large prunes, pitted
9 very thin slices prosciutto cured ham

½ cup of fresh goat's cheese
18 toothpicks

A preheated 425°F oven.

Using a teaspoon, stuff each pitted prune with goat's cheese. Place each prune on a half slice of ham gathering up the ham around the prune and twisting together at the top to form a packet. Pierce through the gathered twisted top with a toothpick and bake in a very hot oven until crisp. Serve warm

CHOUX AU MAQUEREAU FUMÉ ET AU FROMAGE DE CHEVRE
Smoked Mackerel and Goat's Cheese Choux Puffs
Makes 15-20 small puffs

Choux puffs are a versatile appetizer vehicle. My inspiration for fillings often comes from local ingredients. When we're running tours in Provence, for instance, I might stuff them with black olive *tapenade*, a little roasted pepper and some goat's cheese. In Burgundy I serve them warm with garlic butter and snails, and in the Pays Basque, with some fresh ewe's milk cheese and a hint of quince paste.

Here I use smoked mackerel that has been cured with cracked black pepper, but any hot-smoked fish (trout, salmon or bluefish) works equally well. The trick is to find a fresh, mild goat's cheese. I sometimes mix a little *crème fraîche* or heavy cream in with the goat's cheese to get the right creamy texture.

For the choux puffs:
½ cup water
2 tablespoons unsalted butter
½ cup flour
2 whole large eggs
¼ teaspoon salt

For the filling:
½ cup soft fresh creamy goat's cheese.
'Chavroux' is perfect.
Snips of fresh chive, chervil, or dill
3 filets of pepper smoked mackerel

Preheat oven to 375°F.

Put the ½ cup of water in a small saucepan with the butter and salt. Bring to a boil, remove from the heat, and stir in the flour all at once. Mix well until it forms a ball. Put the saucepan back on a low heat and stir the mixture vigorously for a minute or two to dry it out. Remove from heat and let cool five minutes.

Add the eggs to the mixture one at a time beating well after each addition. The mixture should be shiny and smooth, and should hold its shape when dropped from a spoon. Drop the mixture by teaspoonful onto a lightly-greased baking pan. Brush lightly with a little milk and bake for 20 minutes until puffed and golden.

Skin the mackerel filets, pick over carefully for bones, then flake the fish.

When the choux puffs have cooled, split them and put a teaspoon of the cheese mixture, topped with flakes of the mackerel on the bottom of each. Sprinkle on the herb of choice, top with the pastry top and serve.

CANAPÉS DE CREVETTES AU CERFEUIL
Shrimp and Chervil Canapés
Make 18 canapés

I serve this delicious shrimp mixture on thickly sliced and lightly toasted unsweetened brioche rounds. The buttery richness of the brioche works beautifully with the shrimp. This mixture is best served on the day it's made.

18 x 2-inch rounds or squares of good
quality unsweetened brioche

¾ pound cooked small shrimp, peeled and de-veined	1 teaspoon Dijon mustard
1 small shallot minced	1 teaspoon sherry vinegar
2 tablespoons chopped fresh chervil, chives or dill	2 tablespoons canola oil
	4 tablespoons *crème fraîche* or heavy cream
	Fine sea salt and white pepper

Finely chop the shrimp. Combine all the other ingredients in a bowl and whisk together until slightly thickened. Stir in the chopped shrimp. Lightly toast the bread rounds, top with the shrimp mixture and a sprig of herb.

CANAPÉS DE JAMBON CRU A LA POMME VERTE
Cured Ham and Apple Canapés
Makes 18 toasts

Cured ham, green apple and Comté cheese toasted under the broiler... simple as that. A delicious little nibble with a glass of cool white wine.

18 slices of baguette lightly toasted

4 slices of prosciutto-type cured ham
½ cup of Gruyere or Comté cheese diced
½ Granny Smith apple diced

Handful of walnuts lightly toasted and broken into large pieces
1 shallot minced
1 teaspoon of Dijon mustard
4 tablespoons heavy cream
Fine sea salt and black pepper

Preheat the broiler.

Stack the slices of cured ham and slice them into thin strips. Cut across the strips to make a dice.

Mix the diced ham, cheese, apple, walnuts, shallot, mustard, cream, salt and pepper in a bowl. Put a tablespoon of the mixture on each toast slice. Place the toasts on a baking sheet and broil until bubbly. Serve warm.

GOUGERES
Burgundian Cheese Puffs

Gougeres are *the* nibble in Burgundy. That and a *kir* (dry white Aligoté with a dash of *crème de cassis*), and you know you're in Burgundy. Gougeres are cheese puffs made with *pate a choux*, one of those mother recipes of French pastry. It is easy to make and extremely versatile. It's used in desserts such as profiteroles, eclairs and *Paris Brest*, and in savory dishes such as *pommes dauphine* and *quenelles*, it's one of the basics worth having in your repertoire.

Makes 36 Gougeres:

¾ cup of water
5 tablespoons unsalted butter, plus 2 tablespoons to butter the baking tray
Fine sea salt
¾ cup of flour
4 medium eggs at room temperature
½ cup of finely diced *Gruyere* or *Comté* cheese

¼ cup of grated *Gruyere* or *Comté* cheese
Freshly ground black pepper

To finish:
4 tablespoons milk
¼ cup grated *Gruyere* or *Comté* cheese

Preheat the oven to 375°F.

Put the ¾ cup of water in a saucepan with the butter and ½ teaspoon of sea salt. Bring to a boil, remove from heat, and stir in the flour all at once. Mix well until it forms a ball. Put the saucepan back on a low heat and stir the mixture vigorously for a minute or two to dry it out. Remove from heat and let cool five minutes.

Add the eggs to the mixture one at a time, beating well after each addition. The mixture should be shiny and smooth, and should hold its shape when dropped from a spoon. If after the third egg the mixture holds it shape and is not too stiff, think about adding just half or none of the fourth egg. If the mixture is too soft, the 'gougeres' will not puff and hold their shape.

Stir in the diced cheese, ¼ cup of the grated cheese, and the cracked black pepper. Form small balls with a teaspoon, dropping them onto a lightly-buttered baking sheet. Brush them with the remaining milk, sprinkle over the remaining cheese and bake them in the upper third of the oven for 20 minutes until puffed and golden. Serve hot or at room temperature.

WINE

Kir, named after a very hospitable mayor of Dijon, is traditionally made with Aligoté, the 'second' white grape of Burgundy. Originally, the dash of *crème de cassis* was meant to mask the acidity of the Aligoté, and many in Burgundy will serve it to you still as a way of getting away with cheap white wine. But Aligoté has a bad rap; and because of this, it was, until recently, rarely given a decent spot in the vineyards. But when it's planted on a well-exposed limestone slope it produces a lovely wine, floral and fruity with good appley acidity. So pick a good Aligoté and a good *Crème de Cassis*, and you'll have the ideal Burgundian *aperitif.*

COMTÉ MARINÉ AUX ECHALOTES ET AUX HERBES
Marinated Comte Cheese with Shallots and Herbs
Makes 2 cups

Gruyere is a cheese from the Swiss Alps. The term however has come to describe what we would call generically 'Swiss cheese'. As with anything generic, there are many variations and many levels of quality. Generally, these are enormous cheeses—120 pounds at maturity-- made from lakes of cow's milk, cooked, pressed and aged. Quality depends on the milk, of course, but also on the aging. *Comté* is a type of *gruyere* from the Jura, the foothills of the Alps just to the east of Burgundy.

I use a well-aged fruity *gruyere* for this hors-d'oeuvre. You can either serve the mixture on lightly-toasted baguette rounds or on crackers like Carr's Water Biscuits.

Fine sea salt
3 tablespoons dry white wine
2 tablespoons white wine vinegar
2 shallots minced
Freshly ground black pepper
6 tablespoons canola oil

3 tablespoons of chopped chervil (or a mixture of parsley and chive)
2½ cups of coarsely grated *comté* or other Swiss cheese
½ cup lightly toasted walnuts coarsely chopped

In a bowl, dissolve the sea salt in the vinegar. Add the shallots, pepper, and whisk in the oil. Stir in the herbs, grated cheese and walnuts. Let marinate at room temperature for at least ½ hour before serving on the toast rounds.

CANAPÉS DE FOIE GRAS AU CASSIS ET A L'ANETH
Foie Gras with Cassis and Dill
Makes 24 Canapés

Here we combine several Burgundian flavors--the sweet fruit of the black-currant jelly, the exotic spices of the *pain d'épices* and the richness of the *foie gras*—for a surprising burst on the palate.

Look for *foie gras* called *'entier mi-cuit'* , which is the entire fattened liver, molded and partially cooked to give it a creamy, sliceable, pâté-like consistency.

6 thin slices *pain d'épices* spice bread
6 thin round slices of *foie gras*
Blackcurrant jelly

1 tablespoon chopped dill
Fleur de sel, or other flakey sea salt

Lightly toast the spice bread slices. Cut each slice into quarters. Also cut each slice of foie gras into quarters and place on top of the spice bread. Top each with a small dab of blackcurrant jelly. Sprinkle over with the dill and sea salt, and serve.

TARTINES D'OIGNON CONFIT AUX ANCHOIS MARINÉS
Canapés of Slow Cooked Onion and Marinated Anchovy
10 Servings

Marinated fresh anchovies can keep for up to a week in the refrigerator, so the effort that goes into cleaning them is justified. Try them simply with just good bread and lemon, or use them in a fresh salad with thin slices of fennel. The possibilities are endless.

10 slices good quality sourdough bread

For the Onion Confit:
3 red onions peeled and thinly sliced
2 tablespoons extra virgin olive oil
Fine sea salt

For the Marinated Anchovies:
1 pound fresh anchovies
½ cup white wine vinegar
Juice of 2 lemons
Fine sea salt
4 tablespoons extra virgin olive oil
Freshly ground black pepper
2 tablespoons finely chopped flat-leaf parsley

In a small sauté pan with lid, warm the olive oil and add the sliced onions. Season with a little salt, cover and cook very slowly for 30 minutes until the onions are meltingly soft, stirring from time to time. Let cool and reserve.

I find the easiest way to clean anchovies is with your fingers. It makes quick work of it. Use your index finger to gut the fish and then break off the head. Open the fish and flatten with a bit of pressure. Grab the central spine at the head end and pull away from the flesh. Separate the filets, rinse well under cold water and pat dry. Arrange the filets in a shallow dish and pour over the vinegar and lemon juice. Cover the dish and let the lemon and vinegar "cook" the fish in the refrigerator for 4 hours.

Remove the fish from the fridge, drain off the liquid and rinse the filets. Pat dry with paper towel. Arrange again in a shallow dish and drizzle over the olive oil. Season with salt, pepper and parsley, return to the fridge to marinate for a couple of hours and they are ready.

Slice the bread into finger lengths, add some onion *confit* to each piece and top with an anchovy filet. Sprinkle with parsley and serve at room temperature.

The Table

POTAGES
SOUPS

VELOUTÉ D'ENDIVES AUX NOIX ET AUX COQUILLES SAINT JACQUES
Endive Soup with Walnuts and Scallops

CRÈME DE CHATAIGNES AUX CEPES ET AU FOIE GRAS
Chestnut Soup with Cepes and Foie Gras

BOUILLON DE CRESSON AU RAGOUT D'ÉCREVISSES ET GIROLLES
Watercress Bouillon with a Crayfish and Chanterelle Ragout

VELOUTÉ DE NAVETS À LA MIREPOIX D'ESCARGOTS
Turnip Soup with a Mirepoix of Snails

SOUPE AU CRABE AU CURRY ET AUX POMMES VERTES
Curried Crab and Apple Soup

VELOUTÉ DE POTIMARRON AUX TRUFFES ET AU PAIN D'ÉPICES
Butternut Squash Soup with Truffle and Spice Bread Croutons

SOUPE DE PAIN AUX TOMATES ET AUX MOULES
Mussels with Tomato, Bread and White Wine

SOUPE AUX ORTIES
Stinging Nettle Soup

VELOUTÉ DE COURGETTES À LA CRÈME DE CIBOULETTE
Zucchini Soup with a Chive Cream

VELOUTÉ D'ENDIVES AUX NOIX ET AUX COQUILLES SAINT JACQUES
Endive Soup with Walnuts and Scallops
10 Servings

This combination is very autumnal. Scallops, endive and walnuts all find their way into the market stalls here as fall gives way to winter.

The scallops in this recipe are left raw until the last minute, diced and put into warm soup bowls just before serving. Once you ladle over the hot soup they cook on the way to the table, retaining their sweetness.

For the Endive *velouté:*
10 spears of Belgian endive
2 tablespoons unsalted butter
Fine sea salt
1 quart chicken stock
1 cup heavy cream

For the Garnish:
20 large scallops
2 tablespoons chopped tarragon or chervil
2 tablespoons finely chopped fresh walnuts
Espelette pepper
2 tablespoons walnut oil
Fine sea salt

Slice the endive crosswise into half-inch slices. Remove any hard inner core from the pieces.

Melt the butter in a soup pot over medium heat and add the endive. Season with salt and let the mixture cook over a low heat stirring from time to time until the endive is soft, about 10 minutes. Add the chicken stock and heavy cream and continue cooking at a simmer for 20 minutes. Puree the mixture using a hand held immersion blender or a food processor. Taste for salt.

While the soup is cooking prepare the garnish. Slice each scallop in half and then cube them into small pieces.

When ready to serve, divide the scallops among 10 warm shallow soup bowls. Ladle over the hot soup. Sprinkle over the walnuts, tarragon and Espelette pepper. Drizzle over a bit of walnut oil and season with sea salt. Serve hot.

CRÈME DE CHATAIGNES AUX CEPES ET AU FOIE GRAS
Chestnut Soup with Cêpes and Foie Gras
6 Servings

Sweet chestnuts and *cêpes* both start turning up at local markets in October. Their flavors complement one another; and the surprise addition of little nuggets of *foie gras* in each spoonful makes this an elegant seasonal soup.

It's also fairly straightforward to make if you use vacuum-packed, pre-roasted and peeled chestnuts. High quality varieties can be readily found, and will spare you the time-consuming process of roasting and shelling the chestnuts yourself.

If using fresh chestnuts you will need to cut a half-inch crisscross gash on the rounded side of each nut shell with a very sharp knife. Then roast the nuts on a baking tray in a preheated 425°F oven for 15 to 20 minutes, stirring once or twice. The shells will start to crack open. As soon as they are cool enough to handle, quickly remove the shell and peel away the skin. Do not let them cool completely; cold chestnuts are impossible to peel.

2 cups of chestnuts, roasted and peeled
6 cups of chicken stock
¼ cup of heavy cream
1 pound of fresh *cêpes,* stems removed from caps, wiped clean and cut into smallish pieces
4 slices of dense crustless bread, cut into small croutons. French *pain de mie* is perfect.

4 tablespoons of canola or grape seed oil
4 ounces of duck *foie gras entier mi-cuit,* cut into cubes and left at room temperature for 15 minutes before serving the soup
Fine sea salt
Freshly ground white pepper
Sprigs of chervil or flat leaf parsley for garnish

Heat the chestnuts and the chicken stock in a soup pot. Bring to a boil, simmer for 20 minutes and then add the cream. Process the soup in a food processor, blender, or with a hand-held immersion blender until fairly smooth. It's fine to have a few small pieces of chestnut in the soup. Season with salt and white pepper.

While the soup is simmering, sauté the *cêpes* in a large non-stick pan in half of the canola oil. Season with salt and pepper and cook until they release their aroma, but don't brown them. Put them on paper towel to remove any excess fat.

In the same pan, heat the remaining canola oil and sauté the croutons. Season them as well and leave them in the pan to reheat just before serving the soup.

To assemble the soup, divide the *cêpes* and *foie gras* among six warmed shallow soup bowls. Ladle over the hot soup. Garnish with the croutons and chervil sprigs and season with sea salt.

WINE

Not all soups lend themselves to wine combinations, but this one does. Just imagine the texture and the richness of this *velouté*; it cries out for just a little bit of something big and rich, not sweet necessarily, but 'late-harvest': a good Sauternes, or a Tuscan *vin santo*, perhaps. For me, a late-harvest Alsace Riesling from our friend Vincent Stoeffler up in Barr would be ideal. On the other hand, a bone dry Champagne would make a nice contrast.

BOUILLON DE CRESSON AU RAGOUT D'ECREVISSES ET GIROLLES

Watercress Bouillon with a Crayfish and Chanterelle Ragout
10 Servings

For the watercress bouillon:
3 tablespoons unsalted butter
3 leeks cleaned and sliced thinly
8 cups water, light chicken or vegetable broth
4 large bunches fresh watercress
2 tablespoon cornstarch dissolved in
$1/3$ cup water
Fine sea salt
Freshly ground white pepper
2 tablespoons unsalted butter

For the crayfish and chanterelle ragout:
3 tablespoons unsalted butter
¾ pound fresh chanterelle mushrooms cleaned
2 small shallots minced
30 peeled raw de-veined crayfish tails
Fine sea salt
Freshly ground white pepper

To make the watercress bouillon, melt the butter in a soup pot and add the sliced leeks. Let soften for a couple of minutes over medium heat and then add the water or broth. Bring to a boil and simmer for 20 minutes. Puree the soup using a hand held immersion blender or mixer. Return the soup to the pot, whisk in the cornstarch, bring back to a simmer and season with salt and white pepper. Keep covered and warm.

Cut the watercress leaves away from the stems and rinse the leaves under cool water. Bring 4 cups salted water to a boil and blanch the watercress leaves to wilt them. Drain and rinse under cold water to preserve the vibrant green color. Puree in a mixer or processor, adding a little cold water to smooth the purée.

In a sauté pan melt 1 tablespoon of butter and add the cleaned chanterelle mushrooms. Season with salt and cook until the mushrooms release their liquid. Strain the mushrooms and discard the liquid. Return the pan to the heat and melt the other 2 tablespoons of butter. Add the shallots and then the crayfish. Cook them for 3 minutes or so until the crayfish tails turn red, then add the chanterelles back to the pan. Reheat and season.

Reheat the soup and whisk in the pureed watercress and the remaining 2 tablespoons of butter. Taste for seasoning and ladle into warm shallow soup bowls. Add 3 crayfish tails and a spoonful of the chanterelles to the center of each bowl, sprinkle with sea salt flakes and serve hot.

VELOUTÉ DE NAVETS À LA MIREPOIX D'ESCARGOTS
Turnip Soup with a Mirepoix of Snails
10 Servings

This *mirepoix* (a very fine dice of mixed vegetables and herbs), made mostly of carrots, cabbage and mushroom, gives an earthy quality to this autumnal soup, which heightens the mineral, gravely flavors of the snails. This is, in fact, a great vehicle for appreciating the snail.

For the turnip soup:
2 ½ pounds fresh small turnips
6 cups chicken stock
¼ cup *crème fraîche* or heavy cream
Fine sea salt
Freshly ground white pepper
A grating of nutmeg

For the mirepoix:
2 carrots peeled
¼ Savoy cabbage (the curly leaf type)
8 firm mushrooms
4 tablespoons of unsalted butter
3 cloves garlic minced
5 dozen small Burgundy snails ('*helix pomatia*')
2 tablespoons *crème fraîche* or heavy cream
3 tablespoons minced chives or chervil, or both

For the soup: Heat the chicken stock and add the peeled and coarsely chopped turnips. Season with salt, and cook covered over a low heat for 20–25 minutes. Puree the soup in a processor or with a hand-held blender; add the cream, season with the salt, white pepper and nutmeg to taste.

While the soup is cooking, make the mirepoix. Slice the carrots thinly lengthwise, stack and cut into strips, then cut crosswise into a fine dice. Slice the savoy cabbage thinly and then slice crosswise into a fine dice. Slice the mushrooms, and then chop them finely. In one tablespoon of the butter, sauté the mushrooms until all their liquid has evaporated. Transfer the mushrooms to a bowl and reserve. In the same pan melt the remaining butter and add the finely diced carrot, cabbage and garlic. Season with salt, cover and cook over a low fire until soft.

Meanwhile, in a separate pan, heat the escargots with their liquid and enough water to cover just until they come to a simmer. Strain the snails, rinse briefly under cool water and, if they are large, coarsely chop them. Add the snails to the mirepoix with the mushroom mixture and remaining cream. Let this cook covered over low heat for 5 minutes. Reheat the soup. Taste the mirepoix for seasoning and add the herbs. Ladle the hot soup into warm shallow bowls and spoon the mirepoix into the center of each bowl. Serve immediately.

SOUPE AU CRABE AU CURRY ET AUX POMMES VERTES
Curried Crab and Apple Soup
10 Servings

This recipe came with us when we left Annapolis, Maryland back in 1983. It was a favorite on the menu of 'Les Survivants', the restaurant where Dennis and I worked and met. Our mentor, and the owner of the restaurant, Claire Owens, is an inspiration to anyone who loves the kitchen. In the three years I spent cooking with Claire, I worked through a veritable cooking course. Six months as the appetizer girl, a few months on the grill, and then on to the sauté station, it really was a hands-on education. I would listen to Claire talk about her time in Paris at the cooking school 'La Varenne' and her European travels afterwards, and I knew that I had to go and see this for myself.

Back in Annapolis we used lump meat from Maryland blue crabs, of course. Here I use the large Atlantic 'tourteau' crab.

2 medium onions chopped	8 cups chicken stock
3 garlic cloves minced	4 tomatoes peeled, seeded and chopped
3 tablespoons Madras curry powder	1 cup heavy cream
4 medium Granny Smith apples, skin-on and cubed	1 pound lump crab meat picked over for shell
8 tablespoons (1 stick) unsalted butter	Fine sea salt
¼ cup flour	Freshly ground black pepper

In a soup pot, sauté the onions and garlic in butter over medium heat until soft. Add the cubed apple and the curry powder. Cook another 5–8 minutes until the apples have softened a bit. Sprinkle the flour over the apples and mix well. Cook the flour for 3 minutes or so, then slowly add the chicken stock, stirring constantly to avoid lumps (as you would for a béchamel sauce). Once all of the stock has been added, bring the mixture to a boil. Add the tomatoes. Reduce the heat and simmer for 30 minutes. Finish the soup by adding the cream and crab meat. Season with salt and pepper to taste and serve hot.

VELOUTÉ DE POTIMARRON AUX TRUFFES ET AU PAIN D'EPICES
Butternut Squash Soup with Truffle and Spice Bread Croutons
10 Servings

Potimarron is a small pumpkin with a slight hint of chestnut. I like it because it has a slightly sour edge. Use butternut squash rather than pumpkin as a substitute.

This is not meant to be a 'hearty' soup. It is light in texture, allowing the distinct flavors of the squash and truffle to come through. You get a touch of exoticism with the toasted spice bread croutons.

If you can't get truffles, *lardons* of lightly cooked smoked bacon would make a nice addition.

½ cup chilled heavy cream
3 tablespoons minced truffle
4 slices of spice bread, cut into matchstick and cubed
4 tablespoons unsalted butter
2 pounds peeled and cubed potimarron or butternut squash

8–10 cups of water
Fine sea salt
Freshly ground white pepper
2 tablespoons unsalted butter
Fresh sprigs of chervil or chive for garnish

35

Beat the heavy cream until fluffy. Season with salt and pepper and add the minced truffle. Cover and chill. This is best done a few hours ahead of time to allow the truffle flavor to infuse the cream.

Preheat the oven to 375°F. Toast the spice bread croutons lightly. Reserve.

In a soup pot, melt the butter; add the squash and season with salt. Cook for 5 minutes then add the water. Bring to a boil and simmer the soup for 30 minutes. Puree the soup with a hand held immersion blender or in a mixer until completely smooth. Strain the soup through a sieve and return to the pot. Season the soup to taste with salt and white pepper and swirl in 2 table-spoons of butter.

In each shallow serving bowl ladle in the hot soup and add a few croutons. Top with a tablespoon of the truffle cream and garnish with the chervil or chive. Serve hot.

SOUPE DE PAIN AUX TOMATES ET AUX MOULES
Mussels with Tomato, Bread and White Wine
10 Servings

The Italian bread and tomato soup, *pappa al pomodoro*, has always been a favorite on our tours in Tuscany. When we were down near Biarritz recently, running our Pays Basque tours, I came across this combination in a Basque cookbook. Combining the idea of *pappa al pomodoro* with mussels and white wine sounded delicious, and it is.

4 tablespoons unsalted butter
4 cloves garlic minced
2 shallots minced
10 ripe tomatoes skinned and chopped
3 tablespoons of fresh thyme leaves
4 slices of crustless day-old rustic white bread cubed

4 pounds mussels, soaked, cleaned and de-bearded
2 cups dry white wine
Fine sea salt
Freshly ground black pepper
4 tablespoons chopped flat leaf parsley

In a deep saucepan with a tight fitting lid, melt the butter. Add the garlic and shallots, and cook until the garlic starts to turn yellow-gold. Add the chopped tomatoes, thyme and bread cubes, and season with a little salt (carefully because mussels are naturally salty) and freshly ground black pepper. Simmer the mixture for 20 minutes.

Prepare the mussels: bring the 2 cups of white wine to a boil in a large pan with a lid. Boil for 3 minutes; add the mussels, and steam them, covered, just until the shells open. Remove the mussels with a slotted spoon to a large bowl. Pour the broth into a heat-proof glass measuring cup, and allow any grit to settle to the bottom. Add the clear liquid and the mussels to the simmering tomato soup. Bring it back to a simmer and serve hot in warmed shallow soup bowls.

WINE

Wine will work here especially if you think like someone from the coast. Crisp, light, bright and fruity. Burgundy borders on the far end of the Loire, and there you'll find some great sauvignon. Sancerre is the most famous; but just over the border into Burgundy you will find the *appellation* St Bris. There are several good producers; Jean-Hugues and Ghislain Goisot in particular.

SOUPE AUX ORTIES
Stinging Nettle Soup
10 Servings

Here in Burgundy, nettles are an abundant perennial herb--a weed, some would say. High in iron, and containing formic acid and histamines, many consider them a great overall tonic. For cooking, pick them young; use just the first 6–8 leaves. But if they've started to flower, forget it as they will be wooly and bitter. Wear gloves and use scissors when you gather nettles. For this recipe you will need to fill a large salad bowl.

This is one of our early springtime favorites, perfect for when you're coming out of the winter doldrums and craving greens. I first found a version of this recipe in a beautiful book called 'Wild Food' by Roger Phillips. It's full of photographs to help you identify edible plants, and has wonderful recipes in which to use them.

I made this soup often aboard our barge 'Le Papillon' while we were cruising on the Burgundy Canal. I could hop off at a lock with my basket, gloves and scissors, walk along the tow path gathering nettles, and then hop back on at the next lock. People are always surprised at the flavor of nettles, kind of like a cross between peas and asparagus.

I remember one guest (who just happened to be Scottish) making us all laugh by calling out from the dining room, "Ellie, this soup is absolutely delicious… and cheap too!"

2 large yellow onions sliced
2 medium potatoes peeled and cubed
4 tablespoons extra virgin olive oil
A large salad bowl of nettle tops
12 cups of chicken stock
¼ cup *crème fraîche* or heavy cream
Fine sea salt
Freshly ground black pepper

Wash the nettles in a large sink full of cold water, lifting them out with tongs or gloves into a colander to drain.

In a soup pot, sauté the onions and potatoes in the olive oil over medium heat until softened. Season with salt and add the chicken stock. Bring to a simmer and add the nettles. Cook over a low fire for 30 minutes or so. Puree with a hand-held immersion blender or in a food processor. Season the soup with freshly ground pepper, taste for salt. Stir in the *crème fraîche* just before serving.

VELOUTÉ DE COURGETTES À LA CRÈME DE CIBOULETTE
Zucchini Soup with a Chive Cream
Serves 10

This soup should be made with garden fresh small-to-medium-sized zucchini. It couldn't be simpler and the flavor of the squash is absolutely pure and un-adulterated. The vibrant green color comes from leaving the skin on half of the zucchini and <u>not</u> cooking the soup for longer than 15 minutes. The soup can either be served warm or chilled, as you like.

6 cups water
12 small, very fresh zucchini
Fine sea salt
Freshly ground white pepper

For the chive cream:
½ cup heavy cream, whisked to soft peaks
Fine sea salt
Freshly ground white pepper to taste
3 tablespoons minced chives

In a soup pot, bring the water to a boil with a pinch of salt. Wash the zucchini and peel half of them. Cut all the zucchini into 2 inch chunks and add to the boiling water. Let cook uncovered for 15 minutes until the zucchini is soft. Puree the soup with a hand held immersion blender or in a mixer or proces-sor until totally smooth. Season to taste and either chill or serve warm with a dollop of the chive cream on top.

ENTRÉES
STARTERS

RAGOUT DE LEGUMES A L'AIL ET AU JAMBON CROUSTILLANT
Garden Vegetable Ragoût with Garlic and Crispy Ham

ASSIETTE DE PRINTEMPS A LA CRÈME D'AIL ET A L'OEUF POCHÉ
Spring Salad with Garlic Cream, Poached Egg and Ham Powder

SAUMON AUX POMMES VERTES A LA CRÈME DE RAIFORT
Salmon with Green Apples and Horseradish

POELÉE D'ESCARGOTS A LA PUREE DE PERSIL ET AU COULIS DE TOMATE
Sauté of Snails with a Parsley Puree and Tomato Coulis

FILET DE MERLAN AUX COCOS BLANCS ET AU BEURRE D'ANETH
Whiting with White Beans and Dill Butter

SALADE DE LANGOUSTINES ET CELERI RAVE
Langoustine and Celery Root Salad

ŒUFS EN MEURETTE
Poached Eggs in Red Wine

SALADE D'ARTICHAUT ET FOIE GRAS AU PIMENT D'ESPELETTE
Salad of Artichoke, Foie Gras and Espelette Pepper

ESCARGOTS DE BOURGOGNE FORESTIERE
Snails in a Mushroom Sauce

BOUILLON DE MOULES SAFRANÉ AU CERFEUIL ET POTIMARRON
Mussel Bouillon with Saffron, Chervil and a Crush of Butternut Squash

SALADE DE CABILLAUD EN CROUTE DE SESAME
Salad of Sesame-Encrusted Cod

SALADE CHAUDE DE CITEAUX A LA VINAIGRETTE DE NOIX ET VERJUS
Warm Citeaux Salad with a Walnut and Verjus Vinaigrette

FOIE GRAS POELÉ AUX ENDIVES CARAMELISÉES
Seared Foie Gras with Caramelized Belgian Endive

MILLEFEUILLE DE LOTTE ET TOMATES CONFITES A LA TAPENADE VERTE
Napoleon of Monkfish and Oven-Roasted Tomatoes with Green Olive Tapenade

RAVIOLI D'ESCARGOTS DE BOURGOGNE AU BOUILLON VERT
Snail Ravioli in a White Wine, Garlic and Herb Bouillon

FLAN DE PERSIL AU FOIE DE CANARD
Parsley Flans with Sautéed Duck Liver and Warm Sherry Vinaigrette

COQUILLES SAINT JACQUES AU JUS DE PERSIL ET AUX CAROTTES AU GINGEMBRE
Scallops with Gingered Carrots and a Parsley Sauce

MOULES AU FLAN D'ÉPINARDS AU BOURSIN
Mussels in a Boursin Broth with a Spinach and Leek Flan

TOURTEAU AU RIZ SAUVAGE ET TOMATES SECHÉES
Crab with Wild Rice and Sun Dried Tomatoes

SALADE DE CROTTIN DE CHEVRE AUX FEVES ET AUX PETITS POIS
Warm Fava Beans and Peas with Goat's Cheese

RAGOUT DE LEGUMES A L'AIL ET AU JAMBON CROUSTILLANT
Garden Vegetable Ragoût with Garlic and Crispy Ham
6 Servings

It is very important with this recipe that you use only the freshest garden vegetables. I make this salad here in June when new potatoes, green beans, artichokes and fresh spinach are all grown locally and are on my favorite vegetable stalls in local markets.

This spinach sauce is easy to make and brings all the separate flavors of the vegetables together. The fried sliced garlic adds depth and the crispy ham crunch.

1 lemon	1 cup shelled fava or lima beans or fresh
6 small violet artichokes or 3 large	peas
2 cups young fresh spinach leaves	4 thin slices proscuitto-type cured ham
1 pound fingerling potatoes cleaned with	3 garlic cloves thinly sliced
skins left on	6 tablespoons extra virgin olive oil
2 handfuls very slender green beans	1 tablespoons flour
2 stalks celery cut into 1 inch lengths	Fine sea salt
	Freshly ground black pepper

Fill a large bowl with water and squeeze the lemon juice into it. Clean each artichoke. Cut two thirds of the top off with a sharp knife. Pull off the outer leaves and trim, leaving the pale yellow leaves and heart. Scrape out the choke with a spoon. Trim the base and peel the stem, then slice in half or quarters depending on their size. Add to the lemon water.

In a large saucepan of boiling salted water, blanch the spinach until just wilted. Remove with a slotted spoon. Let cool slightly and squeeze with your hands to remove excess water.

Have ready a fairly large baking tray placed in a warm but off oven.

Add the potatoes to the boiling water and cook until tender, about 15 minutes. Remove with a slotted spoon and place on baking tray. Cover with foil and place in the warm oven.

Add the artichoke halves to the boiling water and cook for 8 minutes until tender. Remove with the slotted spoon and add to the potatoes.

Add the green beans to the water and cook for 4 minutes then add the celery and fava beans. Cook for and additional three minutes. Ladle out 1½ cups of the cooking water and reserve. Drain the remaining vegetables and add to the tray. Cover and keep warm.

In a non-stick sauté pan, lightly fry the ham slices until fairly crisp. Remove to paper towel and reserve.

In the same pan, heat 2 tablespoons of the olive oil and in it fry the garlic slices until they turn lightly golden, stirring with a wooden spoon. Don't let them brown or they will be bitter. Pour this oil over the vegetables.

With a hand-held immersion blender puree the spinach with the reserved vegetable cooking water. Heat the remaining oil in the sauté pan and add the flour. Stir and cook the flour for a minute or two and then whisk in the spinach sauce. Cook for 3 minutes and season to taste with salt and pepper.

Have ready six warm plates. Season and gently toss the vegetables. Divide evenly among the plates and drizzle over the spinach sauce. Break the ham into large pieces over the vegetables and serve.

ASSIETTE DE PRINTEMPS A LA CRÈME D'AIL ET A L'OEUF POCHÉ
Spring Salad with Garlic Cream, Poached Egg and Ham Powder
6 Servings

I make this salad when the season's first fresh peas and fat white asparagus stalks arrive on market stalls. A perfect Sunday brunch dish.

It may seem a strange idea to puree proscuitto ham to a powder, but it really does add a unique texture and flavor to this dish.

For the garlic cream:
4 plump garlic cloves peeled
Fresh thyme sprigs
1 cup heavy cream
1 cup milk
4 anchovy filets

2 thin slices proscuitto type cured ham

For the salad:
18 small baby carrots
18 fresh small white spring onions
18 plump green or white asparagus stalks
2 cups fresh shelled peas
1 cup fresh fava beans
2 tablespoons unsalted butter
Fine sea salt

6 large very fresh eggs
Fresh chives or chervil for garnish

In a small saucepan, bring the cream, milk, thyme and garlic cloves to a boil. Reduce the heat and cook at a gentle simmer for 20 minutes stirring occasionally. Add the anchovy filets and cook for an additional 5 minutes. Strain the sauce through a fine sieve pressing on the garlic cloves. Return to the pan and reheat gently when ready to serve.

In a dry non-stick sauté pan, cook the ham slices until crispy. Remove to paper towel and let cool. When cold break the ham into pieces and put into a blender and mix to a fairly fine powder.

In a large sauté pan with lid, melt the butter. Remove from the heat and set aside. Meanwhile in a large pan bring 3 quarts of salted water to a boil for cooking the vegetables.

Prep the vegetables: Peel the baby carrots. Trim the roots and remove the outer skin from the onions. Peel the asparagus and break off the bottom ends. Slice the remaining stalk into two or three pieces. Pod the peas and peel the outer skin off of the fava beans.

Start by cooking the carrots for 5–7 minutes in the boiling water until they are tender. Remove with a slotted spoon and reserve in the pan with the melted butter, cover to keep warm. Add the onions and asparagus to the water and cook until tender. Remove them and add to the carrots. Lastly add the peas to the water and cook for 3 minutes then add the fava beans and cook for an additional two minutes. Drain the peas and favas and add to the other vegetables. Season the vegetables lightly with sea salt and cover the pan to keep warm.

Poach the eggs in plenty of unsalted water with a good splash of white wine vinegar.

Warm six shallow bowls or plates. In the center of each plate place a few tablespoons of the warm garlic and anchovy cream. Divide the vegetables among the plates. Top the vegetables with the poached egg and sprinkle over and around the edge of the plate the powdered ham. Garnish with snips of fresh chive or sprigs of chervil and serve warm.

SAUMON AUX POMMES VERTES A LA CRÈME DE RAIFORT
Salmon with Green Apples and Horseradish
6 Servings

This is a great dinner-party dish that can be prepared ahead of time. You can put individual portions of salmon filet on a baking tray in the refrigerator, ready to pop in the oven. The apple can be sautéed and reheated at the last minute, and the horseradish cream can be kept cool in the fridge until serving time. This recipe can easily be doubled.

1¼ pounds salmon filet
3 Granny Smith apples
2 tablespoons unsalted butter
Juice of 1 lemon
Pinch of cinnamon
Fine sea salt
Freshly ground black pepper

For the horseradish cream:
½ cup *crème fraîche* or heavy cream
2 tablespoons grated prepared horseradish (not the type in cream sauce) or
1 tablespoon fresh horseradish finely grated
1 tablespoon fresh dill minced
Juice of a half lemon
Fine sea salt
Freshly ground black pepper

Skin the salmon filet. Carefully pick out any little bones that may have been missed when the fish was fileted. Slice into six even portions and arrange them on a buttered baking tray, season with salt and pepper. Keep refrigerated.

For the apples: Squeeze the juice of a lemon into a large bowl of cold water. Peel, quarter, and core the apples; then slice each quarter lengthwise into three slices. Stack and slice to the size of thick french fries. Put the apple into the acidulated water to avoid discoloring. Heat 1 tablespoon of butter in a non-stick sauté pan. Drain and pat the apples dry. Sauté them in the butter over a brisk heat for approximately 10 minutes until soft but not disintegrated; don't let them brown, but don't let them steam either. Season with salt, pepper and a pinch of cinnamon.

Pre-heat the oven to 425°F.

Whip the cream or *crème fraîche* until fluffy but not stiff. Add the horseradish, salt, pepper, dill and the lemon juice.

Place the salmon in the preheated oven for 7–9 minutes. You should remove it from the oven when it is still a bit rare on the inside.

Place a bed of apple 'fries' on each warmed plate, top with a piece of salmon and spoon over 2 tablespoons of the horseradish cream. Serve immediately.

WINE

If you don't over-cook the salmon, this dish melts--the salmon into the apple into the horseradish—and if you combine it with a classic 'lesser appellation' Cotes de Beaune white (say, an old-vine Auxey-Duresses from Pascal Prunier-Bonheur or a Savigny-les Beaune from Phillipe Girard), you'll get balance and elegance.

POELÉE D'ESCARGOTS A LA PURÉE DE PERSIL ET AU COULIS DE TOMATE
Sauté of Snails with a Parsley Puree and Tomato Coulis
6 Servings

Quick to execute and full of subtle earthy flavors, this recipe is an argument for keeping a tin of snails on the pantry shelf.

5 dozen medium *escargots de bourgogne* ('helix pomatia')

For the parsley purée:
6 cups of very fresh cleaned parsley
4 tablespoons unsalted butter
Fine sea salt
Freshly ground black pepper

For the sauté:
2 garlic cloves minced
3 shallots minced
¼ cup dry white wine
6 ripe tomatoes peeled, seeded and cubed
4 tablespoons unsalted butter

Place the snails in a sauce pan along with the court bouillon from the tin and add enough water to cover. Bring just to a simmer, drain immediately and rinse under cold water. Reserve.

Blanch the parsley in a large pot of salted boiling water for 4 minutes. Drain and refresh under cold water. Squeeze out any excess water and puree the parsley in a food processor until smooth. In a small saucepan heat the butter gently. Add the parsley and season to taste.

Sauté the garlic and shallots in 2 tablespoons of butter until soft, add the wine, increase the heat and reduce by half. Add the tomatoes and the snails and sauté over a brisk heat for 5–7 minutes, tossing gently. Remove from the heat and swirl in the remaining 2 tablespoons of butter. Season to taste.

Have ready six warm shallow bowls. Place a couple of tablespoons of parsley puree on one side and the snails on the other. Serve at once.

WINE

I always say Chablis with snails; and I'm sure it's because the minerality of Chablis is the most marked of all white Burgundies. But that's no reason not to experiment with other high-mineral white Burgundies. From south to north I'd recommend: Pouilly-Fuisse (here I would include Saint Veran, Viré-Clessé and other Macon-Villages), Saint Romain, Pernand-Vergelesses and Ladoix. And don't forget to look for wines labeled 'Bourgogne Cotes d'Auxerre'. These can be some of the best values in Burgundy.

FILET DE MERLAN AUX COCOS BLANCS ET AU BEURRE D'ANETH
Whiting with White Beans and Dill Butter
Serves 6

This recipe is based on a dish I had years ago in a restaurant near the Dijon market. The combination of fish and beans was unusual: buttery crust, creamy beans, punchy dill. When I made it aboard the Papillon two nights later, it got rave reviews from passengers and crew, so I knew it was a keeper.

Fresh white 'coco' beans still in their pods appear on market stalls in the early autumn. Try to find fresh white haricot beans if possible. When they are in season you can shell them and freeze them for later in the year. Dried beans will not give you the same creamy result; but nevertheless, if you must use dried beans, be sure that they have not been sitting around too long. Even in dried products, freshness counts.

For the beans:
1 pound of fresh white haricot, navy, cannellini or cranberry beans shelled, or 8oz. dried beans soaked over night
Enough water to cover the beans
½ cup heavy cream or *crème fraîche*
Fine sea salt
Freshly ground black pepper

For the dill butter:
4 tablespoons unsalted butter at room temperature
4 tablespoons of chopped fresh dill (the green herb, not the seed)

Squeeze of fresh lemon juice
Fine sea salt
Freshly ground black pepper

6 small filets of whiting, bones removed (a little over a pound)
1½ tablespoons unsalted butter
1½ tablespoons vegetable oil
¼ cup of flour seasoned with salt and pepper
The juice of 1 lemon

Rinse the beans and place them in a small saucepan with water to cover. Add the cream and cook for 40–60 minutes over a medium heat until the beans are just tender and the cream has thickened slightly to a thin sauce-like consistency. Add more water if necessary. When nearly cooked, season the beans with salt and pepper.

Make the dill butter by combining the softened butter with the dill, lemon juice, salt and pepper until fluffy. Keep at room temperature.

Fold the whiting filets in half making a compact piece. Dredge them in the seasoned flour. In a large non-stick sauté pan, heat the butter and oil until foaming. Add the filets with the nicest side down (i.e. not the tail side) in the hot pan and sauté for 4 minutes or so until lightly golden. Flip and continue to cook until just done. Spritz with lemon juice.

Have six warmed dinner plates ready and spoon some of the beans onto each plate. Top with the filets of whiting and dollop over some of the softened dill butter, a little on the fish and a little on the beans. Let the butter melt slightly and then serve immediately.

WINE

This combo, while delicate to the bite, will stand up to a good round white Burgundy. I think of a village Pernand-Vergelesses from Vincent Rapet, young, not too much wood. You could even go red here, depending on the position of the dish in the meal. I see a simple Bourgogne from a good producer in the Cotes de Beaune from a 'feminine' year (as the Burgundians would say).

SALADE DE LANGOUSTINES ET CELERI RAVE
Langoustine and Celery Root Salad
6 Servings

The sweetness of sautéed langoustine on a bed of the tiniest green beans, topped with the nuttiness of slivered celery root: there you have an elegant and delicate salad that can adapt to a simple menu or a formal feast. Simple and fresh, it's French with a twist.

Needless to say, you want to buy langoustines as fresh as possible. As with lobster (they are of the same family) the flesh will go to mush quickly after they die. Properly purchased and prepared, however, langoustine is one the finest delicacies at the fish counter. The English call them 'Dublin Bay Prawns'. Sometimes they are called 'scampi', but there's confusion as 'scampi' can also be giant shrimp.

Large shrimp or crayfish tails could be substituted if the langoustine is unavailable.

For the Vinaigrette:
2 shallots minced
1 tablespoon sherry vinegar
1 teaspoon fine sea salt
1 tablespoon walnut or hazelnut oil
3 tablespoons canola or grape seed oil
1 tablespoon of water
¼ cup fresh coriander or basil chopped
Freshly ground black pepper

1 cup grated celery root
Juice of one lemon

½ pound tiny French green beans
1 teaspoon soy sauce

24 large raw langoustines, shelled and de-veined

Depending on the size of the celery root you may only need to use a third or a half. Grate the celery in a food processor, or better still use a mandolin. You can also use a wide vegetable peeler to make large thin slices that stack and can be cut into long thin julienne strips. Presentation counts! Put the grated celery root in a bowl. Squeeze over the lemon juice and sprinkle over a ½ teaspoon of fine salt. Toss well and let the celery sweat while you are assembling the rest of the salad.

Make the vinaigrette by dissolving ½ teaspoon of fine sea salt in the sherry vinegar. Add the shallots and let them soften for a half an hour or so then whisk in both of the oils and the spoonful of water. Grind in the black pepper and add the coriander.

Peel the raw langoustine tails. Remove the black internal membrane. Reserve.

Blanch the greens beans in salted boiling water for 3 minutes until just tender. Drain and run under cold water to refresh their color. Pat them dry and then toss the beans with the soy sauce and a tablespoon of the vinaigrette.

In a strainer rinse the celery root with cold water to remove salt and lemon. Squeeze out the excess moisture and toss the celery root with a tablespoon of the vinaigrette.

When ready to serve, preheat the broiler. Lightly brush the langoustines with olive oil season with a little salt and pepper and place them under the broiler for 3–5 minutes until just cooked.

Place a bed of green beans on each dinner plate. Top with the langoustine and drizzle over the remaining vinaigrette. Put a fluffy nest of the celery root julienne over the langoustine and serve.

WINE

As for the wine, this dish can be as simple or as elegant as the occasion demands. Imagine what a *Grand Cru* Corton-Charlemagne from the Maison Capitain-Gagnerot would do for a New Year's Eve formal. At the same time, a simple, mineral white, say Saint Romain (Capitain makes a nice one of these, too), would tie the flavors up nicely for a quiet dinner with friends.

CEUFS EN MEURETTE
Poached Eggs in Red Wine
6 Servings

This is the best known of the red wine *meurette* sauce recipes, probably because it is such an unusual combination: poached eggs in red wine sauce. Served with pearl onions and bacon 'lardons' over a garlic crouton, it's a seductive classic. This same *meurette* sauce is also delicious served with fresh water fish.

Your choice of wine for the sauce is important. If you can, use an inexpensive Pinot Noir or maybe Beaujolais. You want fruit; you want good acidity. Color is important, but something like a Cabernet would just be too strong. This sauce reduces very slowly by two thirds its volume, and ends up brilliant and sheeny.

When choosing eggs for poaching, freshness counts. Poach them in plenty of unsalted water (salt thins out the whites) with a splash of white wine vinegar.

For the sauce:
1 bottle of fruity red wine
3 shallots sliced (failing that, an onion)
1 carrot sliced
2 garlic cloves crushed
1 tomato quartered
1 *bouquet garni* (fresh parsley, thyme and bay leaf tied with kitchen twine)
A few black peppercorns
2 cups water

For the thickening agent, a *beurre manie:*
2 tablespoons unsalted butter at room temperature, kneaded with 2 tablespoons of flour

For the garnish:
3 tablespoons unsalted butter
¼ pound of button mushrooms or larger ones quartered: optional
2 slices of ¼ inch-thick un-smoked bacon, cut into *lardons*
24 pearl onions peeled (plunging them into boiling water for 2 minutes makes peeling easier)
1 teaspoon sugar
Fine sea salt
Freshly ground black pepper
Chopped parsley

You will also need croutons that are large enough to hold a poached egg. Cut six two-inch rounds out of good quality dense bread, brush with a little melted butter, season with salt and pepper and bake for 10 minutes in a hot oven.

6 large very fresh eggs

Prepare the sauce: Put the wine into a medium saucepan and bring to a boil. Reduce the heat and ignite the wine with a match. Stand back when you do this as an entire bottle of wine sends up some impressive flames. It should continue to flame for nearly 5 minutes. If it goes out too quickly, try turning the heat up and igniting it again. When the flames subside, add shallots, garlic, tomato, *bouquet garni*, carrot and water. Reduce slowly over a low heat by two thirds (this will take 30–40 minutes). Strain through a fine sieve, pushing on the solids, and reserve in a clean saucepan.

For the *beurre manie*: Knead the butter and flour together in a small bowl. Chill.

Finishing the sauce: In a sauté pan, heat 1 tablespoon of butter with 1 tablespoon of olive oil. Sauté the mushrooms over a brisk heat until their juices have evaporated. Remove the mushrooms from the pan and reserve. Add the *lardons* and pearl onions to the pan, cover and cook over a low fire for 10 minutes until the onions are cooked. Return the mushrooms to the pan, sprinkle over the sugar, deglaze with a small ladleful of the sauce, cover and keep warm while you thicken the sauce.

Reheat the sauce; when bubbling add the chilled *beurre manie* a teaspoonful at a time, whisking until all lumps are dissolved and the sauce naps a spoon nicely. Add the onions, lardons, and mushrooms, and season with salt and pepper to taste. If the sauce is too acidic, add a pat or two of cold butter.

Poach the eggs for 3 to 4 minutes until the whites are set and the yolks soft to the touch.

Warm 6 shallow bowls or plates. Place a crouton in the bottom of each. Top with a poached egg and spoon over the sauce. Garnish with parsley and serve immediately.

WINE

You might think it obvious that you would want to drink the same wine with this dish that you used to make it. Funnily enough, this is not always the best choice. A fruity Pinot will seem tangy against the *meurette* sauce. Egg dishes are notoriously difficult to pair with wine. I've found that I prefer a good round Chardonnay, rich but not oaky, with a hint of minerality like Pouilly-Fuissé or Saint Veran (Denis Barraud makes both really well) or perhaps a village Chassagne-Montrachet from the Domaine Borgeot.

SALADE D'ARTICHAUT ET FOIE GRAS AU PIMENT D'ESPELETTE
Salad of Artichoke, Foie Gras and Espelette Pepper
6 Servings

The espelette cream on the top of this salad pulls all of its flavors together.

½ pound *foie gras entier mi-cuit*
3 large artichoke bottoms cooked
12 slices of smoked duck breast
2 cups watercress leaves
Espelette pepper or very mild
chili powder
¼ cup heavy cream

For the Vinaigrette:
2 tablespoons sherry vinegar
2 small shallots finely minced
½ teaspoons fine sea salt
1 tablespoon walnut oil
2 tablespoons canola oil
1 tablespoon water

Slice the *foie gras* thickly and cut into approximately ½ inch cubes. Do the same with the artichoke bottoms. Stack the slices of smoked duck breast and then sliver into strips.

Whip the chilled cream until it holds soft peaks. Whisk in 2 teaspoons of espelette pepper and chill. Reserve.

In a salad bowl mix the sherry vinegar and shallots with the salt. Add the oil and water and whisk until emulsified. Add the watercress, *foie gras* and artichoke to the salad bowl. Toss lightly and divide the salad among the six serving plates. Top each with a spoonful of the cream and serve.

ESCARGOTS DE BOURGOGNE FORESTIERE
Snails in a Mushroom Sauce
8 Servings

A quick and simple starter that can be prepared well ahead of time. Just do the last step of incorporating the herb butter into the sauce minutes before serving.

Serve these snails in small shallow bowls, piping hot with plenty of crusty French bread.

For the sauce:
¼ pound white button mushrooms
1 tablespoon unsalted butter
2 shallots minced
1 ripe tomato, peeled, seeded and chopped
½ cup heavy cream

5 dozen medium *escargots de bourgogne*
('helix pomatia')

For the herb butter:
¼ pound unsalted butter at room
temperature
The Juice of ½ lemon
2 small shallots minced
2 tablespoons chopped parsley
2 tablespoons chopped chives
Fine sea salt
Freshly ground black pepper

Clean the mushrooms and puree them in a food processor. In a medium sauce pan melt a tablespoon of butter. Add the minced shallots and the tomato. Cook until the shallots have softened, then add the mushroom puree. Increase the heat and cook until the water given off by the mushrooms evaporates. Add the cream, bring to the boil and simmer for 5 minutes. Reserve.

Place the snails into a sauce pan along with the court bouillon from the tin and enough water to cover. Bring to a simmer and drain immediately. Add the snails to the mushroom sauce.

Make the herb butter by mixing together the softened butter, lemon juice, herbs, shallot and salt and pepper.

Ten minutes before serving reheat the snails in the mushroom sauce and let simmer for 5 minutes. Stir in the herb butter tablespoon by tablespoon into the hot snail mixture. Taste for seasoning and serve immediately.

WINE

For all my talk of snails and mineral white Burgundy, here's a dish that's an exception. The mushrooms and the herb butter are voluptuous, and call out for a luscious wine. I see something from the golden triangle of Chassagne Montrachet, Puligny-Montrachet and Meursault, deep and round with a touch of lemon acidity. But don't forget, when you are looking for classic white Burgundy, you'll find great value in the wines from neighboring Saint Aubin, just the other side of the hill and at half the price!

BOUILLON DE MOULES SAFRANÉ AU CERFEUIL ET POTIMARRON
Mussel Bouillon with Saffron, Chervil and a Crush of Butternut Squash
6 Servings

Chervil is used extensively in Burgundian cuisine: as much or more than parsley. It grows well in cool climates. A few chopped sprigs brightens up a finished dish. In this bouillon, it's the chervil that binds the flavors of the mussels and the squash.

Potimarron is not exactly a pumpkin, at least not the Halloween type. It's more a smallish gourd with firm texture and a spicy, slightly "chestnutty" flavour. Butternut squash is a good substitute.

Here in France we're lucky to have the small, sweet *bouchot* mussels from the Normandy coast. Highly-prized and plentiful, no other Atlantic mussel is quite so fine.

Mussels should be alive when you cook them. Storing them in a plastic bag will kill them. Rather, put them in a metal bowl, cover with a damp paper towel and refrigerate them until you are ready to soak, clean and cook them. Discard any mussels that float and do not close up when you soak them.

For the mussel bouillon:
2 pounds small mussels, soaked, scrubbed and de-bearded
Small pinch of saffron threads soaked in ¼ cup boiling water
4 shallots minced
2 cups dry white wine
¼ cup heavy cream
3 tablespoons minced chervil (if unavailable, substitute chives), and several sprigs for garnish
Fine sea salt

For the butternut squash crush:
1½ pounds of cubed fresh butternut squash
4 tablespoons butter
Pinch of freshly grated nutmeg
Fine sea salt
Freshly ground black pepper

For the mussel bouillon: Put the shallots and white wine in a large saucepan. Bring to a boil and after 3 minutes or so add the mussels. Cover and steam the mussels, stirring once or twice until they have opened. Remove them with a slotted spoon to a large bowl. Pour the liquid into a tall glass measuring cup and let any grit settle. Pour the clear liquid carefully back into the pan. Add the saffron to the mussel juice and reduce over medium heat for 5 minutes. Add the cream and chervil. Mussels can be salty, so season to taste. Remove from heat.

Pick three-quarters the mussels from the shells and add them to the bouillon, reserving the rest in the shell for garnish.

For the butternut squash crush: In a large sauté pan with a tight-fitting lid, put the squash cubes in a half cup of water with a small pinch of salt; simmer, tightly covered, for 20–30 minutes. Uncover and stir from time to time until the squash is soft. You may have to add more water to keep the squash from sticking. When soft and dry, add the butter and crush with a fork. Season to taste with salt, pepper and nutmeg. Keep warm, or reheat gently at serving time.

To serve: Have ready six large warm shallow soup bowls. Using a round ring mold, mound a couple of tablespoons of butternut squash crush in the centre of each bowl. Ladle the warm mussel bouillon gently around the squash, and garnish with the reserved mussels in the shell and a few sprigs of chervil.

WINE

Wine with soup is always tricky. You could argue that the mussels make the choice easier, and that a white traditionally served with shellfish would work. However, I think you want a bit of body too. A flinty Sancerre springs to mind...it's almost Burgundian!

SALADE DE CABILLAUD EN CROUTE DE SESAME
Salad of Sesame-Encrusted Cod
6 Servings

It used to be that cod was plentiful, and considered a good, but common fish, with a moist, flaky texture that adapts well to different cooking methods. These days over-fishing has made it almost as rare as salmon used to be. But the same can be said about almost all of the 'noble' fishes. It took a moratorium on rockfish in the Chesapeake to get the levels back. The North Atlantic fishing beds are now struggling with the same issues.

These days, I replace Atlantic cod with pollack (sometimes called pollock and different from Alaskan pollack; what the French call *lieu jaune*). It's from the cod family, very similar in texture; and it's plentiful!

This recipe starts with a *mirepoix*, a tiny dice of vegetables used here to flavor the fish. Always take your *mirepoix* seriously. It's not just for presentation; tiny diced things have more flavor. I don't know why: more surface area in contact with taste buds, maybe.

1½ pounds of cod, or other thick-fleshed fish such as pollack

For the *mirepoix*:
1 small firm red bell pepper
1 small firm yellow bell pepper
3 tablespoons of un-toasted sesame seeds
2 tablespoons olive oil

For the salad:
½ pound mixed salad greens
2 shallots minced
2 tablespoons fresh herbs such as chervil, chives, tarragon or parsley minced
Fine sea salt
Freshly ground black pepper
2 tablespoons sherry vinegar
1 tablespoon sesame oil
3 tablespoons light salad oil, such as canola or groundnut

Trim the fish filets, removing any bones, and cut into 6 even portions. Season with salt and pepper, place on a lightly-oiled baking tray, and chill.

For the *mirepoix:* With a potato peeler, peel the skin off the peppers as best you can. This is done quite easily if the peppers are firm. Slice the peppers lengthwise into very thin strips. Cut strips crosswise into tiny dice. Sweat the pepper dice and the sesame seeds in olive oil over low heat in a non-stick sauté pan covered for 10 minutes until they are soft. Season with salt and pepper. Let cool.

For the vinaigrette: Dissolve the sea salt in the vinegar. Add the shallot and let macerate for 30 minutes to soften. Reserve.

Preheat the oven to 375°F.

Top each fish filet evenly with the pepper and sesame dice. Bake for 8–10 minutes depending on their thickness.

Meanwhile assemble the salad: Whisk the chopped herbs in with the shallots and vinegar. Whisk in the salad oil and sesame oil; season with black pepper. Toss the salad greens with most of the vinaigrette. Place a bed of salad on warmed plates, top with the fish, and drizzle over some remaining vinaigrette. Serve warm.

WINE

Suave and cool is where your wine should be with this dish. The nutty sesame and creamy cod need a little support from behind, so think about a delicate Pinot Noir or a Pinot Noir rosé. They can give you the depth of Pinot fruit without so much concentration, and enough acidity to balance the vinaigrette.

SALADE CHAUDE DE CITEAUX A LA VINAIGRETTE DE NOIX ET VERJUS
Warm Cîteaux Salad with a Walnut and Verjus Vinaigrette
6 Servings

Made by the monks at the Abbey of Cîteaux near Nuits Saint Georges, Cîteaux is one of our favorite Burgundy cheeses. Made from organic cow's milk, it has a true taste of green pastures.

Verjus is made from the juice of unripe grapes, and is often used in Burgundy in place of vinegar. It makes an interesting vinaigrette. I also use it for deglazing a pan after sautéing *foie gras* or to make a sauce after roasting a guinea hen or farm chicken.

If you can't find Cîteaux (its production is positively Burgundian in scale), a good farm-made reblochon is a similar.

I bowl *mâche* (lambs lettuce) cleaned and spun dry
I bunch of white grapes cut in half and seeded
¾ cup of lightly toasted fresh walnuts
2 small shallots minced
I tablespoon *verjus* (or white wine vinegar)

2 tablespoons walnut oil
I tablespoon grape seed or canola oil
Fine sea salt
Freshly ground black pepper
6 slices of sourdough bread, cut in half
½ of a Cîteaux cheese

Preheat the broiler.

Put the *mâche*, grapes and walnuts in a salad bowl. Make the vinaigrette by whisking together the shallots, *verjus*, walnut oil, canola oil, salt and pepper. Lightly toast one side of the bread pieces on a baking tray under the broiler. Turn the bread over and top with slices of the Cîteaux cheese. Place the cheese under the broiler until bubbly and lightly browned.

Toss the salad with the vinaigrette. Divide the salad among 6 dinner plates. Top with the Cîteaux *croûtes* and serve.

WINE

There are certain cheeses that bring out the best in wine, and vice versa. Cîteaux is one of these: red or white, oaked or mineral, delicate or gutsy, all wine goes with Cîteaux; and Cîteaux tastes better with wine: you can hardly go wrong! Although in this recipe the Cîteaux is melted, think also sometime of presenting it as the French would—during the meal, after the main course— or on the all-American *hors d'oeuvre* cheese board.

FOIE GRAS POELÉ AUX ENDIVES CARAMELISÉES
Seared Foie Gras with Caramelized Belgian Endive
6 Servings

If you have never had hot sautéed *foie gras*, you may need an explanation. What you usually find served as a canapé is *foie gras 'mi-cuit'* (as in the recipe for *foie gras* with cassis and dill in the hors d'œuvres section). That is an entire fattened liver, molded and partially cooked to give it a creamy, pâté-like consistency.

This recipe however calls for a fresh, uncooked lobe of *foie gras*, what the French call *'cru'*. It is sliced and sautéed as you would normal liver. But what a difference! Properly seared, it has a crusty outside and a rich, melting interior.

Here in Burgundy there are a few local farms that raise and fatten ducks for *foie gras*. In addition, the duck breast or *magret* is sold fresh and ready to sauté, and the legs are sold as *confit de canard*, conserved their own fat.

Cruising on the Nivernais Canal, we would pass by Madame Duicq's duck farm nearly every week, and would pop by for a peak at the operation. I can understand why some people have the impression that *gavage*, or 'force-feeding' is cruel to the animal; but we have seen time and again that, properly done and on a 'human' scale, no harm comes to the duck. On the contrary, they line up for their turn. Industrial *gavage* may not be pretty; but industrial farming is never good farming anyway.

3 Belgian endives
1 tablespoon unsalted butter
Zest and juice of one lime
1 teaspoon granulated sugar
Fine sea salt

1 fresh duck *foie gras* (approximately 1 pound)
2 small shallots minced
2 tablespoon sherry vinegar
¼ cup port
¼ cup veal or chicken stock
Fine sea salt
Freshly ground black pepper

Rinse the endive and thinly slice crosswise. Push out and discard the hard inner core. In a small sauté pan, melt the butter, add the endive, lime zest and juice, and toss to coat. Sauté over high heat to slightly wilt the endive, then sprinkle over the sugar. Reduce any juice and slightly caramelize the endive. Season with salt to taste and reserve warm.

To clean the *foie gras*, gently separate the two lobes. Using a small knife, carefully remove the thin red blood vessel from each lobe. Cut the lobes on the angle with a very sharp knife into ½-inch thick slices. Season with sea salt and pepper.

Heat a large nonstick sauté pan until it is very hot. Add the *foie gras* slices and sauté for a minute on each side. Remove the slices to a warm platter covered with paper towel to remove excess fat. Keep the slices warm. Pour off all but one tablespoon of fat from the sauté pan. Add the shallots and cook for 30 seconds. Deglaze the pan with the sherry vinegar and port. Let bubble for a minute or two and then add the stock. Reduce until syrupy. Season with salt and pepper to taste.

On six warm dinner plates put down a spoonful of the caramelized endive, top with the *foie gras* and drizzle the sauce around. Serve immediately.

WINE

Classic French cuisine calls for a sauternes here, a deep, rich, honeyed wine to play off of the deep rich flavors of the *foie gras*. And that in fact is a great combo. But try dry, too. Champagne is ideal for a festive occasion. Or a great Meursault, lemony rather than oaky. We love the Meursault from Domaine Moret-Nominé.

MILLEFEUILLE DE LOTTE ET TOMATES CONFITES A LA TAPENADE VERTE
Napoleon of Monkfish and Oven-Roasted Tomatoes with Green Olive Tapenade
6 Servings

I made this dish many times when we were running our tours of Provence. It has all those popular Provencal flavors, and never failed to elicit requests for the recipe. What's more, it's a really striking presentation. So Provencal or not, it gets included in this book. I make it here at home in Burgundy when my garden tomatoes are ripe and flavorful. Make sure that you slice the monkfish thinly and the tomatoes thickly so that when you assemble the Napoleon it stays upright while serving.

If you purchase green *tapenade* for this preparation, make sure that it isn't strongly flavored with garlic and basil, as green *tapenade* often is. Better to use black *tapenade*. Better still, make your own. This recipe makes about 1½ cups, and you will only use half of that in this recipe. Cover the remaining *tapenade* with a thin layer of olive oil and refrigerate. Use in the coming weeks for the 'Croustades of Goats Cheese and Tapenade' in the Hors d'Oeuvres section.

Don't be put off by the long list of ingredients. The recipe is not complicated.

1 pound boneless monkfish filet
Juice of ½ orange
Juice of ½ lemon
4 tablespoons *crème fraîche* or
heavy cream
Freshly ground black pepper

For the tapenade:
6 anchovy filets in oil
2 cups good-quality green olives in brine, pitted
1 tablespoon capers, soaked if salted, or drained if in brine
1 garlic clove minced
4 tablespoons extra virgin olive oil

For the oven-roasted tomatoes:
6–9 large tomatoes
2 tablespoons extra virgin olive oil
Fine sea salt
2 garlic cloves minced

For the vinaigrette:
2 tablespoons balsamic vinegar
Fine sea salt
1 garlic clove minced
1 shallot minced
Juice of ½ lime
1 inch piece ginger, finely grated
½ teaspoon soy sauce
2 tablespoons canola oil
4 tablespoons extra virgin olive oil
1 tablespoon chopped fresh mint, with extra for garnishing

Make the vinaigrette by dissolving the salt in the vinegar. Add the rest of the ingredients, whisk well to combine, cover and let the flavors mingle while you roast the tomatoes.

Preheat the oven to 110° F.

Slice off the top and bottom of each tomato and cut each into thick ¾ inch slices. You will only get 2 or 3 slices out of each tomato. You will need 18 slices in all. Put the slices on parchment paper on a baking tray. Sprinkle over the garlic, drizzle over the oil and season with sea salt. Roast the tomatoes in the low oven for 3–4 hours until they are concentrated but still soft. Discard the skin from the tomato slices. Reserve.

Clean any membrane from the monkfish filet. This is important: otherwise the fish will curl up during cooking. Slice the filet on the angle to make 12 even, thin slices. Reserve on a plate in the refrigerator.

Make the *tapenade* by placing all the ingredients except the oil in a food processor. Process to form a thick paste and then slowly add the oil in a steady stream. Season to taste with freshly ground black pepper.

Put half the *tapenade* mixture in a small saucepan and add the orange and lemon juice. Stir in the cream and taste for seasoning.

When ready to serve gently reheat the tomatoes in a low oven. Gently heat the *tapenade* cream until just warmed through.

In a large non-stick pan heat a tablespoon of olive oil and sauté the monkfish slices for 1 minute on each side.

On six flat dinner plates put a tablespoon of the *tapenade* cream in the center. Top with a tomato slice then a piece of fish then another tomato slice another piece of fish and end with a tomato slice. Whisk the vinaigrette and drizzle a tablespoon or two of dressing around the Napoleon. Garnish with the mint and serve warm.

RAVIOLI D'ESCARGOTS DE BOURGOGNE AU BOUILLON VERT
Snail Ravioli in a White Wine, Garlic and Herb Bouillon
6 Servings or 24 raviolis

The consumption of snails in Europe has a long and, admittedly, dry history covering, according to some, 10,000 years and any number of species. So when purchasing snails it is important to look on the label for the taxonomic names. There are really only two species worth looking for: the Burgundy snail (called *'helix pomatia'*) and the petit gris from Provence (called *'helix aspersa'*). Almost anything else is likely to be an Asian slug, and not a snail at all.

These ravioli take some time to prepare, but are worth the effort. They can be made ahead of time and kept refrigerated on a trays lined with parchment paper, covered with dishtowels in single layers for up to 4 hours. The pasta should be rolled out on the thinnest setting of your pasta machine. This makes the ravioli very delicate.

For the pasta:
2 cups of all-purpose flour or, better,
typo 00 Italian pasta flour
2 large eggs
2 egg yolks
A small amount of milk, just to bind the dough

For the bouillon:
6 garlic cloves peeled
2 shallots sliced
1 celery stick sliced
1 carrot sliced
1 onion minced
1 *bouquet garni* (fresh parsley, thyme and bay leaf tied with kitchen twine)
3 cups dry white wine
3 cups water
Small pinch of sea salt and 6 black peppercorns

For the filling:
5 dozen small *escargot de Bourgogne* ('helix pomatia')
½ pound of white mushrooms
2 garlic cloves minced
1 shallot minced
1 tablespoon unsalted butter
½ cup heavy cream
2 tablespoons unsalted butter at room temperature
2 tablespoons finely minced fresh herbs such as chervil, chive or parsley
Fine sea salt
Freshly ground black pepper

For the garnish:
2 tomatoes peeled, seeded and diced
1 tablespoon unsalted butter
A handful of fresh chervil chopped, or minced chives

Make the pasta by putting the flour, whole eggs, and egg yolks in the bowl of a food processor. Process. At the end of 30 seconds or so, the mixture should form into fairly small crumbs. (It should not form a ball. If it does, the mixture is already too wet, and you will need to add a little more flour.) Once you have the small crumb consistency, drip in the milk, drop by drop, with the machine still running. You want a paste that is neither crumbly nor sticky, but that holds together when pinched. Knead into a ball and let the pasta rest, covered with plastic wrap for at least 30 minutes.

Make the bouillon: Combine all the ingredients in a saucepan. Bring to a boil and then simmer uncovered for 1½ hours. Strain through a fine sieve into a small pan, pressing on the solids. You should have about 2 cups of bouillon. Reserve the bouillon.

Place the snails in a small saucepan with the liquid from the tin and enough water to cover. Bring just to a simmer, drain immediately and rinse under cold water. Reserve.

Make the filling by chopping the mushrooms in a processor almost to a puree. In a sauté pan, cook the garlic and shallot in butter until soft. Add the mushrooms and season with salt and pepper. When the mushrooms have given off all their liquid and are fairly dry, add the drained escargot and the cream. Cook and let reduce until almost dry, 5 minutes or so. Off the heat stir in the butter and herbs. Taste for seasoning, let cool, chill and reserve.

Divide the pasta dough into 2 equal portions and roll each out to the thinnest setting on a pasta machine. Lay a sheet of pasta on a work surface and cut into 4 inch squares. Place a teaspoonful of the mushroom mixture in the center of each square making sure to include two *escargots* in each spoonful and bring two opposite corners of the dough together to form a triangle. Press the edges firmly to seal. Bring a large pan of salted water to a boil. Drop in the ravioli and cook for 4–5 minutes.

While they're cooking, bring the bouillon to a simmer. Add the tomato and swirl in the butter. Taste for seasoning. It should have a fairly sharp flavor of wine to complement the richness of the filling.

Serve the ravioli hot in shallow warmed bowls with a ladleful of the bouillon and garnish with the chopped chervil or chives.

WINE

One of the surest wine and food combos is snails with Chablis. I call the flavor 'gravelly'. You can't miss. We have several favorite producers: Nathalie and Gilles Fevre; the Domaine du Chardonnay; Jean-Claude Oudin; Gerard Tremblay; Sylvain Mosnier; Didier Picq, to name but a few.

FLAN DE PERSIL AU FOIE DE CANARD
Parsley Flans with Sautéed Duck Liver and Warm Sherry Vinaigrette
6 Servings

This recipe goes back to our early barging days when we were first cruising the Burgundy Canal and cooking for 20 people.

These parsley flans are so delicate they shimmy. The duck livers are rich and creamy. And the warm sherry vinaigrette brings the flavors together into a clean, simple, elegant starter that you can have on the table easily inside an hour.

You will need six small ½ cup ramekins or round small oven-proof coffee cups.

For the parsley flans:
3 cups of parsley, picked, cleaned and spun dry in a salad spinner
2 whole eggs
I egg yolk
I cup milk
I cup heavy cream
I teaspoon of fine sea salt, and a pinch of nutmeg
Unsalted butter at room temperature for the ramekins

For the livers:
12 fresh duck livers (or substitute large chicken livers)

I teaspoon butter and I teaspoon oil for the sauté
Fine sea salt
Freshly ground black pepper

For the vinaigrette:
3 tablespoons sherry vinegar
8 tablespoons light salad oil such as canola or groundnut
2 tablespoons minced shallots
I tablespoon chopped fresh herbs such as chives or chervil
Fine sea salt
Freshly ground black pepper

Preheat the oven to 325°F.

Prepare the flans: In the bowl of a food processor reduce the parsley to a fine mince. Add the eggs, the yolk, cream, milk, salt, and nutmeg to the processor and blend for 30 seconds. Butter the individual ramekins and divide the mixture evenly among the 6 ramekins. Place them in a baking dish and pour boiling water around the outside until it comes halfway up the sides of the ramekins. Lightly cover with foil and bake for 25–30 minutes until slightly puffed. You can keep them warm in the water bath while sautéing the liver.

Make the vinaigrette by dissolving the salt in the vinegar. Add the shallots and let them macerate for 30 minutes to soften. Whisk in the oil, pepper and herbs.

Clean and trim the livers. Slice them thinly on the angle (3 slices per liver).

Warm your dinner plates. Heat the oil and butter in a sauté pan until the butter foam subsides. Sauté the liver slices in the hot butter, seasoning with salt and pepper. Cook them until just done, slightly pink is good. Turn them on to paper towel to drain off any excess fat.

Shake the parsley flans from side to side vigorously, and turn them out onto the plate. Divide the liver slices among the plates, spoon over some vinaigrette and serve.

WINE

Even though we're not quite at the richness level of *foie gras* here, your wine selection might take a hint from what is traditionally served with such rich dishes. Generally you'll see either stark dry Champagne or, on the other end of the spectrum, a rich, even sweet wine, like Sauternes. Bearing in mind that here we have the additional consideration of the vinaigrette, and also the egg in the flans, my instinct is to lean towards the richer wine. Not sweet, necessarily, but fruity and buttery. Try a late-harvest Alsace grape like Pinot Gris, or a voluptuous Vouvray from the Loire.

COQUILLES SAINT JACQUES AU JUS DE PERSIL ET AUX CAROTTES AU GINGEMBRE
Scallops with Gingered Carrots and a Parsley Sauce
Serves 6

Sea scallops are one of my winter favorites. They come into season in October, and you find them on the market stalls fresh in their shells. The fishmonger will open and clean them for you, and return them to their shells ready to be stuffed with a little herb butter and grilled or baked. Simple, sweet and delicious.

This is a delicate recipe. The parsley sauce calls for lots of fresh parsley. It is extremely light and sets off the sweetness of the scallops.

I'll say it again: don't buy frozen scallops. Whereas fresh scallops seize and brown well, remaining tender and juicy in a hot sauté, frozen scallops break down, give off lots of liquid and go tough and chewy. It's best to wait until scallop season! Here they are available from October right through till springtime.

For the parsley sauce:
4 cups parsley picked and thoroughly cleaned
Ice water for refreshing the parsley
Fine sea salt
2 tablespoons unsalted butter
1 teaspoon cornstarch mixed with
2 tablespoons of water

4 medium carrots
1 tablespoon olive oil

1 inch piece peeled ginger root
¼ cup dry white wine
¼ cup heavy cream
Grated zest of ½ orange
18 large sea scallops
A little olive oil and butter for the sauté
Fine sea salt
Freshly ground white pepper

In salted boiling water, blanch the parsley for 4 minutes. Drain and immediately plunge it into the ice water to refresh its vibrant green color. Drain and blend it in a blender to a smooth puree. You may need to add a little water to do this. Put the puree into a small saucepan and reserve.

Wash, peel and cut the carrots into matchstick pieces. Not too thinly as you want them to cook in the wine yet still have some crunch when served.

In a non-stick pan heat the olive oil over medium heat and add the carrots and grated ginger. Toss and season with salt and white pepper. Add the wine and let bubble for a minute or two to cook off the alcohol. Cover the pan with a lid reduce the heat to low and cook for 8–10 minutes until the carrots are nearly cooked through but still have some bite. Add the cream and orange zest, cover and keep warm off the heat while you sauté the scallops.

Slowly heat the parsley sauce and whisk in the cornstarch. Bring to a boil, season with salt and white pepper to taste. Remove from the heat and swirl in the butter.

Warm six serving plates or shallow bowls.

Remove the 'muscle' from the side of each scallop. Heat a large non-stick sauté pan over high heat. Add a little olive oil and butter. When hot and sizzling add the scallops and sear for a scant minute on each side. Season with salt and white pepper.

Place a few tablespoonfuls of the parsley emulsion on one side of each warm plate. Put a small bed of carrots on the other side and arrange the scallops on top. Pour over any juices from the scallop pan and sprinkle over some sea salt flakes.

> WINE
>
> If you are thinking holidays, think Champagne. It would work really well here, bringing out the sweetness of the scallops. Otherwise, I think you want to be going with something not too round. A well-made *village* Puligny-Montrachet has a lemony acidity that would accent the dish. Once again, I think of the Domaine Borgeot to get the style right.

MOULES AU FLAN D'ÉPINARDS AU BOURSIN
Mussels in a Boursin Broth with a Spinach and Leek Flan
6 Servings

'*Du pain, du vin, du Boursin*' It's one of those perennial French products, doyen of the cocktail party scene. The fact that it mounts the generations must mean it has something essentially French about it. Here there's no *baguette*, no *chopine* of red wine. But because Boursin melts beautifully, it's the base of a tasty mussel soup served with a little spinach flan. Roquefort cheese also works well in this recipe.

For the spinach flans:
You will need six small ½-cup ramekins or oven-proof coffee cups.

1 tablespoon butter at room temperature, for buttering the ramekin molds
½ pound fresh spinach
2 whole eggs
¾ cup milk

¾ cup heavy cream
1 teaspoon salt and a pinch nutmeg

For the mussels:
3 pounds small mussels, soaked, cleaned and de-bearded
2 large shallots minced
2 cups dry white wine
2½ ounces Boursin cheese with herbs (not the garlic one)

Preheat the oven to 325°F.

Bring a large pot of salted water to a boil. Blanch the spinach for 3 minutes. Drain and refresh under cold water. Squeeze out excess liquid and put the greens in a food processor. Add the eggs and puree the mixture. Stop, add the milk, cream, salt and nutmeg, and then blend until smooth. Spoon the mixture into the buttered molds to fill them ¾ full. Place the molds in a baking dish, and pour boiling water around the outside of the molds until it comes half way up the sides. Bake for about 20–25 minutes until puffed. Prick the center of one of the molds with a toothpick: if it comes out clean, they are done. Remove the molds from the water bath and let them settle for 5 minutes.

While the flans are baking, prepare the bouillon. Bring the wine and shallots to a boil in a large pan with a lid. Boil for 3 minutes; add the mussels, and steam them, covered, until the shells open. Remove the mussels with a slotted spoon to a large bowl. Pour the broth into a heat-proof glass measuring cup, and allow any grit to settle to the bottom. Pour the clear liquid back into the saucepan, add the cream, bring to a boil and, off the heat, add the Boursin cheese. Whisk the sauce, taste for seasoning and reserve off the heat. Pick the mussels (saving a few in their shells for garnish) and return them to the broth. Reheat when ready to serve.

Have six warmed shallow soup bowls ready. Shake the ramekins vigorously from side to side to loosen the flans. Gently unmold them into the center of each bowl. Ladle the mussel bouillon around the flans, garnish with the reserved mussels, and serve.

WINE

This dish makes me think of an old-style classy Paris bistro night-out-on-the-town place that's loud and boisterous and fun. In my script, they are drinking Sancerre, a flinty Sauvignon that will go really well with the mussels and the creaminess of the sauce, as well as with the earthiness of the spinach.

TOURTEAU AU RIZ SAUVAGE ET TOMATES SECHÉES
Crab with Wild Rice and Sun Dried Tomatoes
6 Servings

There's one thing that still makes me home-sick after all these years: crabs. I grew up on the Chesapeake Bay, and summer was crabs. We caught them by the bushel. So I have a natural soft spot for this combination of warm crabmeat, wild rice and sun-dried tomatoes, set off with a pinch of espelette pepper.

¾ cup wild rice
2 tablespoons olive oil
2 tablespoons unsalted butter
8 sun dried tomatoes diced
2 shallots minced
I pound fresh crabmeat
Zest of one organic lemon
Fine sea salt
Espelette pepper to taste

For the sauce:
½ cup heavy cream
½ cup light chicken stock
2 teaspoons soy sauce
I tablespoon unsalted butter

Heat the oil in a non-stick pan over medium heat. Add the rice and toss to coat. Cover the rice with 2 cups of water. Bring to a boil, reduce to a simmer and cover and cook over low heat until the rice is tender.

Put the two tablespoons of butter in a sauté pan over medium heat. When it starts to foam add the tomatoes and shallots and warm through. Add the crabmeat and lemon zest. Mix in the cooked rice gently and season with salt to taste. Cover and keep warm.

In a small sauce pan heat the cream with the stock, bringing it to a bare simmer. Add the soy sauce and butter, and whisk until foamy.

Serve the crab mixture in warmed bowls with a few tablespoons of sauce around in each bowl and sprinkle over the espelette pepper. Serve warm.

SALADE DE CROTTIN DE CHEVRE AUX FEVES ET AUX PETITS POIS
Warm Fava Beans and Peas with Goat's Cheese
6 Servings

This simple springtime salad should be made from garden fresh vegetables at their peak. Use top-quality extra virgin olive oil, *fleur de sel* salt and freshly ground quality pepper to make the ingredients sing.

Crottin de chevre are small, round, goat's milk cheeses that range from soft and fresh to aged and dense (hence the name: look it up!). Here in Burgundy most goat's cheese comes from the Morvan natural park, with some produced further south near the Beaujolais region. The upper reaches of the Loire valley also have an important production. Look for a semi-fresh cheese, what the French call *mi-sec,* that has developed a white crust, but is still tender to the touch. At this stage they are perfect for baking.

Another variation of this peasant-style salad replaces the goat's cheese with a poached egg.

2 cups shelled and skinned fava beans	6 *crottin de chevre*
2 cups shelled peas	Extra virgin olive oil
2 scallions thinly sliced	Fine sea salt
6 thin slices proscuitto or other cured ham	Freshly ground black pepper

Preheat the oven to 375°F.

Bring a large saucepan of salted water to the boil.

Bake the *crottin* on a non-stick baking tray for 10–12 minutes until soft and semi melted. Keep warm.

While the cheese is baking, heat a large non-stick sauté pan over high heat and drizzle in a little olive oil. Sauté the ham slices for 1 minute on each side until crispy and reserve on paper towels to remove any excess fat.

Cook the fava beans and the peas in the salted water until just tender and then drain.

On six warm plates scatter the fava and peas. Sprinkle over the spring onions and season with salt, pepper and olive oil. Place the cheese baked-side facing up on the salad. Break the ham slices into large pieces and place on the salad. Serve warm.

PLATS
MAIN COURSES

CABILLAUD ET POMMES DE TERRE AU GINGEMBRE ET PINOT EPICÉ
Cod with Ginger Potatoes and Spiced Pinot Noir

SANDRE AUX TROMPETTES DE LA MORT AU JUS DE TOPINAMBOUR
Pike-Perch with Black Trumpet Mushrooms and a Jerusalem Artichoke Sauce

MERLU ET MOULES DE BOUCHOT AU BEURRE D'ESCARGOT
Hake and Mussels in a Garlic and Parsley Broth

POULET AUX ÉCREVISSES
Chicken with Crayfish

LAPIN A LA MOUTARDE DE DIJON
Rabbit with Dijon Mustard

TENDRONS DE VEAU BRAISÉS AU VIN BLANC
POMMES DE TERRE ECRASÉES A LA MOUTARDE ET CIBOULETTE
Veal Breast Ribs Braised in White Wine with a Crush of Mustard Chive
Potatoes

TOURNEDOS DE VEAU AUX LANGOUSTINES ET AUX PISTACHES
HARICOTS VERTS HACHÉS
Medallions of Veal with Langoustine and Pistachio with Chopped Green
Beans

MAGRET DE CANARD ET SA TOURTE BOURGUIGNONNE
RADIS GLACÉS ET PURÉE DE CELERI
Duck Breast with 'Duck Burgers' Celery Root Puree and Glazed Radishes

MAGRET DE CANARD AU JUS DE COING
Duck Breast with a Quince Paste Sauce

ONGLET A L'EPOISSES
Flank Steak with an Epoisses Sauce

FILET DE BOEUF A LA MOELLE AUX GIROLLES ET PINOT NOIR
Tournedos with Marrow and Chanterelles in a Pinot Noir Sauce
Gratin Dauphinois

CARRÉ D'AGNEAU A LA CRÈME D'AIL ET CITRON
LEGUMES ROTIS
Rack of Lamb with Garlic and Lemon Cream and Roasted Root Vegetables

CREPINETTES D'AGNEAU AU FROMAGE DE CHEVRE
Bacon Wrapped Lamb Noisettes with Goat Cheese

FILET DE BICHE AU CASSIS ET GRATIN DE CHOUFLEUR AU
GINGEMBRE
Venison Filet with Blackcurrants and a Ginger Cauliflower Gratin

DAUBE DE SANGLIER ET POMMES DE TERRE RAPÉES
Wild Boar in Red Wine with a Burgundian Potato Galette

CABILLAUD ET POMMES DE TERRE AU GINGEMBRE ET PINOT EPICÉ
Cod with Ginger Potatoes and Spiced Pinot Noir
6 Servings

As I mentioned in an earlier recipe, cod used to be plentiful. These days, over-fishing has made it almost as rare as salmon used to be.

So I replace Atlantic cod with pollack (sometimes called pollock and different from Alaskan pollack; what the French call *lieu jaune*). It's from the cod family, very similar in texture; and it's plentiful!

I've always liked sheeny red wine sauces with fine flaky fish. Here exotic spicing mingles with a heady wine sauce and ginger potatoes to bring texture, flavor and color into sharp focus.

The red wine sauce and the ginger potatoes can be made ahead of time and reheated, so that the only thing left to do is cook the fish before serving.

6 x 6 ounce pieces of thick un-skinned cod-like filet

For the ginger potatoes:
6–8 medium yellow-fleshed potatoes (such as Yukon Gold)
4 tablespoons unsalted butter
A 2-inch piece of fresh ginger grated
Fine sea salt
Freshly ground black pepper
(Optional) 1 medium pickled lemon minced

For the sauce:
1 carrot finely chopped
1 stick of celery finely chopped

1 onion finely chopped
3 tablespoons unsalted butter
¼ teaspoon ground allspice
¼ teaspoon ground cloves
A grating of fresh nutmeg
1 tablespoon Madras curry powder
1 bottle of Pinot Noir
1 teaspoon sugar
2 cups of fish or chicken stock
Fine sea salt
Freshly ground black pepper

For the thickening agent, a *beurre manie*: 2 tablespoons of unsalted room temperature butter kneaded with 2 tablespoon of flour. Chill and reserve.

Scrub the potatoes and put into a saucepan covered with cold water. Add a pinch of salt bring to a boil and cook until the potatoes are just done. Drain and let cool completely. When cool, remove the skins and cut the potatoes carefully into ½ inch dice. Melt the 4 tablespoons of butter in a large non-stick pan. Add the grated ginger and cook over a low heat for 5 minutes. Add the potato cubes and cook an additional 5 minutes. Reserve.

Make the sauce: Melt the 3 tablespoons of butter in a heavy saucepan large enough to hold all the ingredients. Add the carrot, celery and onion and a

80

teaspoon of salt. Cook over a brisk heat until the vegetables start to brown (6–8 minutes). Add the spices and cook for 2 minutes, then add the red wine, stock, and sugar. Bring to a boil, reduce the heat to medium-low, and slowly reduce the sauce to about 2 cups. Strain through a fine sieve into a clean saucepan; keep warm.

Preheat the broiler of your oven. Brush the fish pieces with melted butter and season with salt and pepper on both sides. Put the fish on a heavy baking tray lined with foil skin side up. Put the fish in on the second rack down from the broiler and cook for 6–8 minutes depending on the thickness of the cod pieces. If you don't have a broiler, bake the fish in a preheated 425° F oven.

Gently reheat the potatoes. Add the minced pickled lemon (if you choose) and season to taste.

Finish the sauce by whisking the *beurre manie* a teaspoon at a time into the simmering sauce to thicken. Whisk until all lumps are dissolved and the sauce naps a spoon nicely. Taste for salt.

On six warmed plates place a bed of potatoes, top with the fish, skin side up, and spoon the sauce around.

> WINE
>
> These are fairly exotic spices for a Burgundian red wine sauce, but have no fear; Pinot Noir takes them on squarely. In fact, I would say make the sauce with a regional appellation Bourgogne, and kick up the level to a village Volnay, or a Savigny-les Beaune for the table. These villages will give you delicate, almost floral Pinot notes. The Boillot cousins in Volnay and the Girard brothers in Savigny all make great wine.

SANDRE AUX TROMPETTES DE LA MORT AU JUS DE TOPINAMBOUR
Pike-Perch with Black Trumpet Mushrooms and a Jerusalem Artichoke Sauce
6 Servings

Sandre is arguably the finest of the fresh water fishes. It got its English name (though the English themselves also call it 'zander') because it looks like a perch and hunts like a pike. It also has the blue-white flesh of the perch, and the flavor of the pike, but without the million little bones.

If you can't find the 'pike-perch', substitute a delicate white-fleshed fresh-water fish such as perch, or walleye pike.

The 'trumpets of death' (as the French translates) are the dark-brown to almost-black *craterellus* mushroom. I've seen them called 'horn of plenty' or 'black trumpets' in English. They are plentiful, fairly inexpensive and incredibly tasty.

I like to serve the fish on a bed of braised leeks and Belgian endive (recipe below).

For the sauce:
8 firm fresh Jerusalem artichokes
scrubbed and peeled
2 cups water
Pinch of fine sea salt
Ground white pepper
Fresh chives or chervil minced
3 tablespoons heavy cream

3 tablespoons unsalted butter
2 tablespoons extra virgin olive oil

1 cup seasoned all purpose flour
2 pounds of *sandre* filet, de-boned, skinned
and cut into six portions

For the mushrooms:
1 pound trompette mushrooms, bottoms
removed and picked over
2 tablespoons unsalted butter
Fine sea salt
Freshly ground black pepper

Slice the artichokes and put them in a small saucepan with the water and a pinch of salt. Bring to a boil and then simmer for 10 minutes. Puree in a mixer or with a hand held immersion mixer. Season with white pepper and salt to taste and reserve warm.

In a large heavy-bottomed sauté pan heat the butter and oil until foaming. Dredge the fish pieces in the seasoned flour patting off the excess flour with your hands and put them in the sizzling hot fat. Sauté until browned nicely on one side; carefully turn with a spatula, trying not to break up the pieces.

If the mushrooms are gritty dunk them in a large bowl of water and remove immediately and drain on paper towel. If they are fairly clean just wipe them with wet paper towel. While the fish is cooking, in another sauté pan cook the mushrooms in butter and season to taste.

Reheat the sauce and add the heavy cream. With a hand-held immersion mixer, blend again to foam the cream, or whisk until frothy. Taste for seasoning and add the minced chives or chervil.

When the fish has browned, squeeze a little lemon juice over each piece.

On six warmed shallow bowls, place a bed of the leeks and endive. Top with a piece of the fish and then the mushrooms. Put a few tablespoons of sauce around and garnish with chive sprigs.

For the braised leeks and endive:
3 medium leeks
4 Belgian endive spears
2 tablespoons unsalted butter
Fine sea salt and white pepper

Remove most of the dark green top of the leeks. Cut them on an angle into ½ inch slices. Soak in a large bowl of cold water to remove any grit.

Rinse the endive and slice into 1 inch pieces lengthwise. Push out and discard the hard inner core.

Bring a medium saucepan of the lightly salted water to a boil and add the leeks and endive. Let blanch for 2 minutes then drain. Add the butter to the warm saucepan. Return the vegetables and season. Cover and reheat the vegetables when ready to serve.

> ## WINE
>
> This is a recipe that will support a dry, steely white or a light, fruity red. I think Chablis goes really well yet at the same time, I do like a light Pinot with some of these flaky fresh-water fish. Why not try both as an experiment? It's astounding how much a wine can effect your appreciation of a dish.

MERLU ET MOULES DE BOUCHOT AU BEURRE D'ESCARGOT
Hake and Mussels in a Garlic and Parsley Broth
6 Servings

The 'beurre d'escargots' is the garlic and parsley butter that we serve our snails with in Burgundy. No snails here, though!

Use any white-fleshed fish for this dish. I like hake; but you will find different fish where you are than I get here. Make this in the spring when fresh peas and asparagus are plentiful in the local markets.

We are spoiled here in France with the wonderful and plentiful Bouchot mussels from the Normandy coast. But when cooking in the states I have also found King Edward Island mussels to be delicious. Small clams would also work in this dish.

6 x 6 ounce pieces of thick un-skinned hake filet

2 pounds mussels soaked, scrubbed and de-bearded
I cup dry white wine

For the Garlic Parsley Butter:
4 tablespoons softened butter
2 small shallots minced
I clove garlic minced

4 tablespoons chopped fresh parsley
Fine sea salt

16 fresh slender green asparagus spears, stalk bottoms broken off and peeled if needed
2 cups fresh peas
2 cups pearl onions peeled
2 tablespoons extra virgin olive oil
I garlic clove peeled and crushed slightly

In a large soup pot with lid add the wine. Bring to a boil and after a couple of minutes add the mussels. Cover the pot and steam open the mussels. Remove from the heat and lift out the mussels with a slotted spoon. Pour the mussel juice into a Pyrex cup and allow any grit to settle out. Cover the mussels to keep them warm.

In another saucepan bring 2 quarts of salted water to a boil. Add the peas, asparagus and onions. Cook for 5 minutes, drain gently, return to the pan and cover to keep warm.

Pour the reserved mussel juice into a small saucepan leaving behind any gritty residue and reduce the juice by $\frac{1}{3}$. Add the parsley butter and emulsify with a hand held immersion blender or whisk in the butter so the mixture is frothy.

In a large non-stick sauté pan with lid, heat the olive oil until fairly hot. Season the fish on both sides with salt and pepper and add to the pan skin side down. Add the crushed garlic clove and cover the pan. Reduce the heat and let cook for five minutes.

Have ready six large shallow warm bowls. In each put the fish pieces in skin side up. Add some of the mussels to each and divide the vegetables among the bowls. Ladle over the parsley juice and serve immediately.

PLATS/MAIN COURSES

85

POULET AUX ÉCREVISSES
Chicken with Crayfish
6 Servings

Chicken and crayfish dishes have been part of the culinary repertoire of towns along the River Saône for centuries. Still today, you can see flat-bottomed fishing boats moored in the shallows, square-framed net rigs dangling from davits. Although there is not much commercial fishing anymore, amateur fishermen can still take enough crayfish to satisfy local demand.

You are unlikely to find Breese birds easily outside of big city markets. But free range, organically fed chickens are now readily available and worth their price. The difference between a real bird and one of those swollen yellow things you find at the supermarket is, well, it's what this is all about.

The French way of portioning a chicken is a bit different to what you see elsewhere. In addition to the leg, thigh and breast portions, they cut $\frac{1}{3}$ off of each breast leaving it attached to the wing, making the wings presentable pieces as well.

A plump 4 ½ pound chicken, portioned into six servings (see note above)
4 tablespoons unsalted butter
2 tablespoons cooking oil
Fine sea salt
Freshly ground white pepper
24 fresh crayfish
3 shallots minced
2 carrots diced
1 onion diced
3 garlic cloves crushed
½ cup dry white wine
1 tablespoon tomato paste
1 cup chicken stock
¼ cup *crème fraîche* or heavy cream
2 tablespoons chopped chervil

Heat the 2 tablespoons of butter and the oil in a heavy sauté pan with lid that will hold the chicken pieces comfortably in one layer. Over medium heat gently brown the chicken pieces until golden. Season the chicken with sea salt and pepper and after 5 minutes or so remove the chicken pieces to a platter and reserve.

Drain off most of the fat from the pan and then add the shallots, carrots, onion and garlic. Let the vegetables sweat for 5 minutes and then deglaze with the white wine. Let this bubble up and scrape the bottom of the pan well to loosen any coagulated cooking juices. Reduce heat to medium. Add the crayfish, partially cover the pan and cook them for 8–10 minutes (depending on size). Remove the crayfish from the sauté pan with tongs and set aside on a platter. Leave the vegetables and juice in the pan.

Add the tomato paste and the chicken stock to the pan. Return the chicken skin side up and simmer, partially covered over a low heat for 30 minutes. While the chicken is cooking, remove the crayfish tails and peel them. Remove the black vein in the tails. Set the crayfish heads aside, reserving six for garnish.

When the chicken is tender, transfer it to a warm platter and keep it warm. Skim any fat off the cooking liquid. Add the remaining crayfish heads to the sauce and crush them slightly with a pestle. Simmer the sauce for 5 minutes more, then strain it through a fine sieve, pressing on the solids. Return the sauce to the pan and add the heavy cream and chervil. Taste for seasoning and return the chicken to the pan to reheat gently. Add the crayfish tails just before serving. Serve each chicken portion with 4 crayfish tails. Garnish the plates with the reserved crayfish heads. Serve with pasta, rice or pearl barley.

WINE

Living on a canal barge, you see the world differently. A practical notion once struck me that a good way of matching wine with a dish is to think about where the recipe originates. Here, the crayfish takes you down to the river. In Burgundy wine country, this would mean you are cruising on the Saône through the Maconnais or on the Yonne up around Chablis. Both of these areas produce mainly white wine with a high mineral content. River valleys, limestone, it all makes sense. So choose a Macon-Villages white or a Pouilly-Fuisse if you are dreaming of the Saône; and if your boat's on another river, maybe a Côte d'Auxerrois or Chablis; any of these will work.

LAPIN A LA MOUTARDE DE DIJON
Rabbit with Dijon Mustard
6 Servings

We eat a lot of rabbit at home in Burgundy. As much, I'd say, as we eat chicken. It's lean, tender meat, cooks quickly and is really versatile. Here, for instance, I roast it with a mustard basting. It is succulent; and I'll serve it with rice or fresh pasta, even braised pearl barley—something to absorb the tangy mustard sauce.

I also often serve rabbit in a classic Burgundian red wine *meurette* sauce.

I fresh rabbit (about 3 pounds) cut into 8–10 serving pieces	I cup chicken stock
¼ cup vegetable oil	½ cup heavy cream or *crème fraîche*
2 tablespoons unsalted butter	2 tablespoons fresh tarragon or basil chopped
½ cup Dijon mustard	Fine sea salt
½ cup dry white wine	Freshly ground black pepper
I onion finely chopped	

Preheat the oven to 375°F.

In a Dutch oven or large ovenproof sauté pan, heat the oil and butter until foaming. Add the rabbit pieces (don't crowd the pan; do two batches if necessary) and brown thoroughly. Remove the rabbit from pan and drain off any fat. Brush the rabbit pieces with half of the mustard, and season with salt and pepper. Put back in the pan and roast uncovered in the oven for 15 minutes. Pour the wine into the pan and baste the rabbit pieces. Return to the oven and continue cooking for another 15 minutes. Sprinkle over the chopped onion and add a little more wine if the pan has gone dry and cook for an additional 10 minutes. Remove the rabbit pieces to a warm platter cover with foil and keep warm in an off oven.

Place the roasting pan over a high heat, and bring the juices to a boil, scraping up any browned bits. Add the stock and reduce for a couple of minutes. Finish the sauce by adding the cream and tarragon. Let thicken a bit and then whisk in the remaining mustard to taste. Season with salt and pepper and return the rabbit pieces to the sauce to warm through.

> WINE
>
> Here's a chance to drink a young red from the Côte de Nuits, something charming from Chambolle-Musigny or Morey Saint Denis. Choose a village wine over a more elaborate *premier cru*, you'll find that the brightness of the young fruit plays off the succulent juices and tangy mustard of this dish.

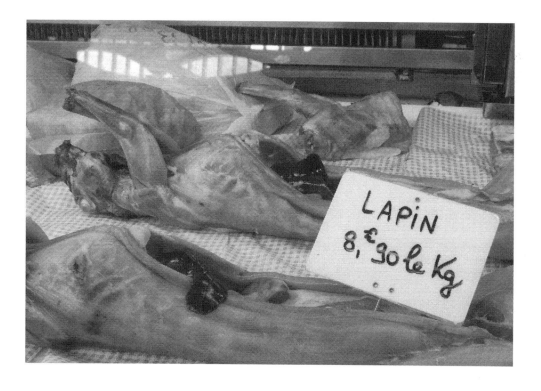

TENDRONS DE VEAU BRAISÉS AU VIN BLANC
POMMES DE TERRE ECRASÉES A LA MOUTARDE ET CIBOULETTE
Veal Breast Ribs Braised in White Wine with a Crush of Mustard Chive Potatoes
6 Servings

Veal *tendrons* are thick-cut strips of veal breast; in France, a very popular and fairly inexpensive cut. They are superb for braising, extremely tender and flavorful. Essentially you are looking for veal spareribs cut from the center of a veal breast. Ask the butcher to cut the breast meat parallel to the bones into strips just like spareribs, and each sparerib into 3 pieces crosswise.

Braised slowly in white wine until the meat falls from the bone and served over crushed potatoes with mustard and chives (recipe follows) it makes a very satisfying dish indeed. Like all braised dishes, this one is even better reheated the next day.

4 pounds veal breast, cut into 4-inch-long and 2-inch-wide spareribs, fat trimmed	*Bouquet garni* made of bay leaf, parsley and thyme
3 tablespoons olive oil	Fine sea salt
2 carrots coarsely chopped	Freshly ground black pepper
1 stick celery coarsely chopped	2 cups dry white wine
2 small onions coarsely chopped	2 cups veal or chicken stock

You can either braise the veal on top of the stove on its lowest setting (the liquid should really just quiver) or in a 280°F oven.

In a heavy-bottom pot with a tight-fitting lid, heat the olive oil. When hot, add as many pieces of veal as will fit in one layer without crowding the pan. It is important to sear the meat without 'stewing' it. Brown the pieces very well on all sides. This will take awhile, and you may have to do two batches. Take your time, though: be careful not to burn the bottom of the pan, but be sure the meat is well-browned. Remove the veal to a plate, season with salt and pepper, and reserve. In the same pan add a little more olive oil and cook the carrots, celery, and onions over a medium heat until they are also well browned. Deglaze the pan with the white wine, bring to a boil and reduce a little. Add the stock, *bouquet garni*, and then return the meat to the pot and cover with the lid. Put the pot in the oven (or reduce the heat on the stove

90

top to its lowest setting), and braise the meat for 1½–2 hours or until the meat is very tender.

Lift the meat out of the braising liquid and reserve. Strain the liquid through a fine strainer, pressing on the solids. Skim the liquid of any fat that may rise to the surface and then reduce the liquid by half over a brisk heat. Season to taste with salt and pepper. Return the meat to the liquid to reheat gently.

POMMES DE TERRE ECRASSÉES A LA MOUTARDE ET CIBOULETTE
Crushed Potatoes with Mustard and Chives

12 small Yukon Gold or other waxy type potato
4 tablespoons unsalted butter
4 tablespoons *crème fraîche* or heavy cream

3 tablespoons full-grain mustard
4 tablespoons minced chives
Fine sea salt
Freshly ground black pepper

Peel the potatoes and put them in large pot of cold salted water. Bring to a boil, reduce the heat and cook the potatoes until they are easily pierced with a knife. Drain them and then return them to the warm pot. Add the butter, *crème fraîche*, mustard and chives. Season with salt and pepper, and crush them gently with a large fork, leaving large chunks. Mix well. Serve hot.

WINE

This is one of those 'feel good' dishes, so your wine should make you feel good too! Something big and juicy, but not too fancy. I'd go for a simple red 'Bourgogne', from a great producer. We love Rapet Pere et Fils. In the end, it's who makes the wine that counts. While it's always a joy to have big name *appellations* aging away in the cellar, the simpler wines from great winemakers are the real pleasures of living in Burgundy. They are more accessible young, and often some of the best deals going! Look for *appellation* 'Bourgogne' in both red and white.

TOURNEDOS DE VEAU AUX LANGOUSTINES ET AUX PISTACHES HARICOTS VERTS HACHÉS

Medallions of Veal with Langoustine and Pistachio with Chopped Green Beans
6 Servings

The langoustines here could easily be crayfish, lobster meat, or crabmeat. All have a sweetness that plays off the pan-roasted crusty-but-tender veal. I also like to throw in a vegetal edge with a very fine chop of green beans.

Ideally you want your butcher to cut you 1-inch thick rounds from the center of the filet.

You will need a large heavy sauté pan that will easily hold all six tournedos in one layer, and that can be transferred from the stove top to the oven.

6 center cut 1-inch thick veal medallions, 2 pounds in total	Fine sea salt
	Freshly ground black pepper
5 tablespoon unsalted butter	1 tablespoon chopped tarragon
1 tablespoon oil	10 thin slices of *pancetta* or thin cut strips of unsmoked bacon
18 langoustine tails, peeled and de-veined	
1 cup dry white wine	½ cup green, peeled, raw and unsalted pistachios, coarsely chopped
1 cup veal or chicken stock	

Pre-heat the oven to 425°F.

In a large sauté pan heat 2 tablespoon of butter with the oil over high heat. When the butter foams, add the veal medallions and sear completely on both sides, browning the meat well. Season with salt and pepper and put into the preheated oven for 8 minutes.

Remove the veal from the oven and let the meat rest on a warm platter loosely covered with foil.

Pour off any fat from the pan and put the pan over high heat. Deglaze with the wine and reduce by half. Add the stock and reduce by half. Strain the sauce into a small saucepan, add the tarragon, season and keep warm.

While the wine and stock are reducing, bake the *pancetta* slices on a baking tray in the oven until crisp. Pat off any excess fat and reserve the slices warm.

In a non-stick sauté pan heat 2 more tablespoons of butter over high heat. Add the langoustine and season with salt and pepper. Cook for 3 minutes until just done. Reserve warm. Strain any juices into the veal sauce. Mount the sauce with 1 tablespoon of butter and adjust the seasoning.

Place the tournedos on warmed dinner plates. Top each tournedos with 3 langoustines and a slice of *pancetta*. Sprinkle over the chopped pistachios and spoon the sauce around. Garnish with the chopped green beans.

HARICOTS VERTS HACHÉS
Minced Green Beans

½ pound of green beans, topped and tailed	Freshly ground black pepper
Fine sea salt	2 tablespoons unsalted butter

Blanch the beans in a pot of salted boiling water for 4–5 minutes. Keep them slightly crispy. Plunge immediately into ice water to refresh. Drain the beans and put them into a food processor. Pulse chop the beans until you have a fairly fine chop. Do not puree them.

Heat the butter in a non-stick pan and warm the beans gently. Season and serve hot.

WINE

You want nice high notes from a juicy Pinot here. I immediately think Savigny-les Beaune. Look out for either of the Girard brothers (Jean-Jacques or Phillipe) You want to avoid the more animal, leathery aspects of Pinot, so choose your vintage carefully too. Burgundians class vintages as either 'masculine' or 'feminine' (often leading to other discussions). I'd say 'feminine' here.

MAGRET DE CANARD ET SA TOURTE BOURGUIGNONNE
RADIS GLACÉS ET PURÉE DE CELERI
Duck Breast with 'Duck Burgers' Celery Root Puree and Glazed Radishes
6 Servings

The *magret* is the breast of a duck that has been fattened to make *foie gras*. It is dark, rich meat without being gamey. Since *foie gras* production has been 'democratized' in France (meaning that a lot more farmers have gone into *foie gras* production because it pays), there is consequently a lot of *magret* produced as well. Here in Burgundy, we are more likely to find *magret* than normal duck breast.

But if *magret* is unavailable, choose large, plump duck breasts. You will need four breasts in all, one for the *pâté* and half a breast each for the six servings.

I like to serve this duck with glazed radishes and maybe a celery root puree or a sauté of Jerusalem artichokes.

For the duck pate:
½ pound chilled puff pastry
I duck breast with all skin removed
¼ pound good quality pork sausage meat
I whole egg
Pinch fresh thyme
I teaspoon Worcestershire sauce
Fine sea salt
Freshly ground black pepper
2 tablespoons milk for the glaze

For the sauce:
2 cups good quality chicken stock
¼ cup sugar
⅓ cup balsamic vinegar
2 tablespoons cold unsalted butter
I tablespoon cornstarch mixed with 2 tablespoons cold water
Fine sea salt
Freshly ground black pepper

Preheat the oven 350°F.

Make the duck pâté: Cube one duck breast and place it in the bowl of a food processor. Pulse to grind to a semi-fine texture (do not puree). Stop the processor and add the pork sausage meat, the egg, thyme, Worcestershire sauce, salt and pepper. Pulse again until well combined. Roll out the puff pastry to a 1/8 inch thickness. Cut out 12 3-inch rounds with a pastry cutter or a glass turned upside down and a sharp knife. Prick 6 of the rounds with a fork and arrange them on a baking sheet. Spoon 2 tablespoons of the pâté mixture on top of each of the rounds, smoothing it out evenly. Score the remaining 6 rounds with a sharp knife in a decorative pattern. Place these on top of the pâté mixture. Brush with the milk and bake in the oven for 20 minutes until golden.

While the pâtés are baking begin the sauté of the duck breasts. Score the skins of the breasts for even browning. Lightly oil a heavy sauté pan and put over a medium heat. When hot, cook the duck breasts skin side down for 6–8 minutes until skin is evenly browned. Drain off most of the fat and turn the breasts to continue cooking either in the oven or on the stove top for another 5–8 minutes depending on their thickness and how well done you like duck meat. Season the breasts with salt and pepper and reserve warm, covered loosely with a piece of foil.

Pour off all but a tablespoon of the fat from the sauté pan. Over medium heat caramelize the sugar in the pan, don't let it burn, and when caramelized add the balsamic vinegar. Stand back: the fumes from the vinegar are strong. Let this bubble up for a minute then add the chicken stock. Reduce for 5 minutes, and then add the cornstarch to thicken. Swirl in the butter, strain into a small sauce pan and season to taste with salt and pepper.

Cut each duck breast in half and slice each half into slices. On each warm plate put a pâté round and the duck slices. Spoon the sauce over the duck, garnish with the vegetables and serve.

PUREE DE CELERI
Celery Root Puree

1 large celery root	Fine sea salt and white pepper
6 tablespoons unsalted butter	

Peel the celery root. Cut into large chunks, rinse and place immediately into cold water to cover. Add a good pinch of salt and bring to a boil. Cook for about 20 minutes until the celery root is soft. Drain and puree in a processor with the butter and season with the salt and pepper to taste. Reserve warm.

RADIS GLACÉS
Glazed radishes

24–30 very fresh round red radishes with their greens	Fine sea salt
2 tablespoons unsalted butter	Freshly ground black pepper
2 tablespoons granulated sugar	1 tablespoon walnut or sesame oil

95

Remove the greens, wash them and let them dry on a towel.

Clean the radishes and put them in a sauce pan that will just hold them in one layer. Add water to come halfway up the sides of the radishes. Add the butter and sugar. Cook uncovered over a medium heat until the water evaporates. Roll the radishes in their syrup and season with salt and pepper.

Heat the walnut oil in a non-stick pan and stir fry the greens. Season and serve them as a bed for the glazed radishes.

WINE

You definitely do not want a 'jammy' Pinot on this one. The sauce here is rich and a little 'sweet and sour', so you want a red with gumption, a good bit of acidity and maybe even a bit rustic. I'd go looking in Santenay, or maybe Auxey-Duresses. These are two villages from the southern part of the Cotes de Beaune that deserve more attention. Young producers like Pascal Borgeot in Santenay or Pascal Prunier-Bonheur in Auxey are masters of bringing out the *'terroir'* of their village wines. And the quality level puts these 'lesser-known' *appellations* into the same league as their more famous neighbors.

MAGRET DE CANARD AU JUS DE COING
Duck Breast with a Quince Paste Sauce
6 Servings

These days quince paste is easily found in specialty shops, usually at the cheese counter. It is traditionally served sliced to accompany Spanish Manchego cheese. In this recipe it is turned into a luscious sauce to serve with sautéed duck breast. Great with black beans, wild rice, or this pearl barley pilaf (see recipe below). Add a crisp green vegetable like watercress or blanched snow peas.

3 large plump duck breasts	Pinch of ground cinnamon
¼ pound quince paste, cut into small pieces	Freshly ground black pepper
6 tablespoons water	3 tablespoons extra virgin olive oil
2 cloves garlic peeled	Juice of 1 lemon
1 teaspoon coarse sea salt	1 tablespoon sherry vinegar

In a small saucepan melt the quince paste in the 6 tablespoons of water by heating and whisking until the paste dissolves and forms a smooth loose sauce without lumps. Let cool slightly.

In a small bowl pound the garlic with the sea salt to form a paste. Add the cinnamon, black pepper and olive oil. Add this to the warm quince sauce. Whisk in the lemon juice and sherry vinegar. Taste for seasoning.

Score the skins of the duck beasts for even browning. Lightly oil a heavy sauté pan and put over a medium heat. When hot, cook the duck breasts skin side down for 6–8 minutes until the skin is evenly browned. Drain off most of the fat and turn the breasts to continue cooking either in the oven or on the stove top for another 5–8 minutes depending on their thickness and how well done you like duck meat. Season the breasts with salt and pepper and reserve warm, covered loosely with foil and left to rest 5 minutes before slicing.

Re-warm the quince sauce adding any juice that has accumulated in the duck pan. Cut each duck breast in half and slice each half into slices. On each warm plate spoon a pool of the sauce and top with the duck slices. Serve with your vegetable of choice.

PEARL BARLEY PILAF

6 Servings

2 tablespoons extra virgin olive oil
I small onion diced
I stalk celery minced
I teaspoon ground cumin
I teaspoon fine sea salt

2 cups pearl barley
5 cups chicken stock or water
2 tablespoons full grain mustard
3 tablespoons heavy cream

Pre-heat the oven to 375°F.

In an oven-proof braising pan with a cover, melt the butter and sauté the onion until soft. Add the cumin, celery and barley and sauté for another 3 minutes, coating the barley. Add the stock or water and bring the mixture to a boil. Add the salt. Cover with parchment paper and a lid or foil. Put into the oven for 35–40 minutes, checking after 25 minutes for doneness and to make sure the barley still has some liquid left to absorb adding more if needed. Once tender add the mustard and heavy cream and taste for seasoning.

ONGLET A L'EPOISSES

Flank Steak with an Epoisses Sauce
6 Servings

You have to understand, we think Epoisses is one the greatest cheeses in the world. I include this recipe because the combination, simple as it is, is just too good.

Epoisses cheese is produced in our local town ….Epoisses! It's a round disc-shaped cow's cheese with a distinctly orange skin (having been being brushed with *marc de Bourgogne* to keep it from forming a rind) that is generally ready to eat after about 6 weeks of aging.

The family-run restaurant in the center of town, *'La Pomme d'Or',* devotes an entire tasting menu to this wonderful cheese. They serve a sautéed hanger steak (what the French call *'onglet'* or *'la piece du boucher'*—literally, the piece the butcher keeps for himself!) with this simple, delicious Epoisses sauce.

You may have to do some explaining to get an American butcher to give you this exact piece of beef—there is only one in every cow. It's located just below the tenderloin. If you do find it, it is best 'butterflied' against the grain. It's not the most tender cut, but is really flavorful. Failing this, choose your preferred cut.

6 x 8 ounce steaks of your choice
Freshly ground black pepper
2 tablespoon unsalted butter
2 tablespoon vegetable oil
6 shallots minced

I cup dry white wine
½ of an Epoisses cheese
2–4 tablespoon heavy cream (optional)
Fine sea salt

To cook six steaks you will need two very large heavy-bottomed sauté pans and two burners capable of bringing the pans to a very high heat in order to sear and cook the meat properly. Otherwise, you will have to sauté the steaks in two batches.

Season the steaks lightly with fresh pepper and heat your pans with the butter and oil until foaming. Cook the steaks to your liking and season them with sea salt. Put them on a warm platter covered very loosely with foil and let rest while you make the sauce.

Add the minced shallots to the pan and let them soften a bit. Deglaze the pan with the wine and let it bubble and reduce for 2–3 minutes, scraping up all the brown bits stuck to the bottom of the pan. Reduce the heat to a simmer and add the Epoisses cheese, letting it melt into the wine. Season with black pepper and taste for salt (Epoisses itself can be a bit salty, so be careful with the salt). Add any of the steak juices that have accumulated on the platter, and if you think the sauce is too tart add the heavy cream. You can also thin the sauce if you like with some water if it seems too thick.

Serve the steaks immediately with the sauce drizzled over, some snips of fresh chives and good home fries or roasted potatoes as accompaniment.

WINE

This is a bistro style plate, so think along those lines for the wine. A slightly chilled Beaujolais Villages would be great. Or a simple young Bourgogne Rouge. Something 'quaffable'!

FILET DE BOEUF A LA MOELLE AUX GIROLLES ET PINOT NOIR
Tournedos with Marrow and Chanterelles in a Pinot Noir Sauce
Gratin Dauphinois
6 Servings

To claim that the distinctive white Charolais steer is as much a symbol of Burgundy as are its famous wines might be stretching the point a bit; but anyone who has ever visited this pastoral region will have come away with an image of graceful white herds on grassy hillsides.

WINE

This is a classic of French cuisine, and is very wine friendly. You can hardly go wrong with a gutsy Pinot Noir. And if you want, this would be a good time to pull out an aged bottle.

The 'tournedos' is cut from the center of the filet. Ask you butcher to cut them 2-inches thick.

I've given below my favorite recipe for *gratin dauphinois* that you could serve on the side if you wish.

6 6-ounce filet mignons, cut 2-inches thick
6 pieces of beef marrowbones cut into
2-inch lengths
3 shallots minced
1 tablespoon unsalted butter mixed with 1
tablespoon cooking oil (for the sauté)
2 tablespoons unsalted butter for finishing
the sauce

For the mushrooms:
½ pound of chanterelle mushrooms
2 tablespoons unsalted butter
Fine sea salt

2 tablespoons heavy cream (optional)
2 tablespoons minced chives

For the sauce:
3 cups of Pinot Noir red wine
1 carrot sliced
A bay leaf
1 small tomato chopped
1 crushed garlic clove
1 small onion chopped
Fine sea salt
Freshly ground black pepper
3 tablespoons unsalted butter

Soak the marrowbones in cold water for several hours to remove any traces of blood. Bring a saucepan of water to a simmer and poach the marrowbones for 5 minutes. Remove, let cool, and push the marrow out of the bones. Slice each piece into two and reserve on a plate.

For the sauce: put the red wine in a saucepan and bring it to a boil. When the wine boils, ignite it with a match. Attention: the evaporating alcohol from the wine is very flammable. Continue to boil until the flame dies out, about 3–5 minutes. Add 1 cup of water, the carrot, bay leaf, tomato, garlic, and onion. Reduce heat to a simmer, and reduce the sauce by two thirds. Push through a fine sieve, pressing hard on the solids. You should have a little over a cup of sauce. Reserve.

Clean the chanterelles thoroughly. Sauté them in a little bit of very hot butter, season with salt and, when they release their liquid, strain them. Add a little more butter to the pan and return the mushrooms, season with salt, pepper, cream and the chives.

Preheat the oven to 350° F.

In a heavy sauté pan, large enough to hold all the steaks in one layer without crowding them and that can also fit in your oven, melt the tablespoon of butter in the tablespoon of oil. Heat over a high flame. When the foaming of the butter subsides, sauté the steaks for 2 minutes on each side to sear them. Transfer the pan to the oven and continue cooking for about 6 minutes for rare and 8 minutes for medium-rare. Transfer to a cutting board, cover loosely with foil and allow to rest.

Drain off the fat from the pan. Add the minced shallots and let them brown for a minute or two and then sprinkle them with a pinch of sugar. Add the red wine reduction to deglaze the pan. Bring to a boil, reduce the heat to low and add the marrow slices. Cook slowly for 4–5 minutes and without stirring, swirl in the cold butter bit by bit until it is absorbed. This will help thicken the sauce. Season with salt and pepper.

Slice each tournedos in half; top each rosy half with a piece of marrow and spoon the sauce around the meat. Garnish with the mushrooms and serve.

GRATIN DAUPHINOIS
Potato and Cream Gratin

Many recipes for *gratin dauphinois* include grated cheese or call for it to be sprinkled over the top. Not here. I find the combination of dairy products with the starchiness of the potatoes produces a faint but distinct flavor of cheese, but there's none added.

I clove garlic
3 tablespoons softened unsalted butter
1½ pounds of Yukon gold or Russet potatoes
Fine sea salt

Freshly ground black pepper
Pinch of grated nutmeg
1¼ cups whole milk
1¼ cups *crème fraîche* or heavy cream

Pre-heat the oven to 375°F.

Crush the clove of garlic and rub the bottom of a large shallow baking dish well with the garlic. Discard the garlic, and butter the dish with half of the softened butter.

Peel the potatoes and slice them thinly. While you are slicing the potatoes bring the milk and cream to a boil in a large non-stick pan. Reduce the heat and add the potato slices. Cook over a low heat stirring well from time to time to keep the potatoes from sticking to the bottom of the pan. Season with salt, pepper and nutmeg. Simmer the potatoes for 15 minutes until they are about half-cooked. Spoon the potato mixture into the buttered dish and dot with the remaining butter. Bake for 30 to 40 minutes until bubbly and brown.

CARRÉ D'AGNEAU A LA CRÈME D'AIL ET CITRON
LEGUMES ROTIS
Rack of Lamb with Garlic and Lemon Cream and Roasted Root Vegetables
6 Servings

Rack of lamb is truly a special occasion cut. This recipe works equally well with a shoulder roast or leg of lamb which are certainly more affordable.

You will need two racks of 9 chops each, giving you three chops per person. Ask your butcher for racks weighing about 3 pounds each. Have them 'French trim' the racks to the eye of the meat, with all fat removed and bones cleaned. Split each rack into three pieces with three chops each.

I like to serve the lamb with roasted root vegetables (see recipe below).

The lemon cream and vegetables can be made ahead of time and reheated while the lamb is resting after roasting.

6 portions of rack of lamb, described above
2 tablespoons olive oil
6 sprigs rosemary
Fine sea salt
Freshly ground black pepper

For the lemon garlic sauce:
2 shallots chopped
4 garlic cloves peeled
I cup dry white wine
Juice of 2 lemons
2 cups chicken stock
I cup heavy cream
2 tablespoons chopped fresh rosemary
Fine sea salt
Freshly ground black pepper

Pre-heat the oven to 425°F.

Rub the lamb pieces with the olive oil and season with salt and pepper. Place a sprig of rosemary on each, and roast the lamb for 15 minutes (longer, if you prefer lamb a little more cooked). Let the meat rest lightly covered with foil to keep warm for 10 minutes before serving.

To make the sauce, place the chopped shallots and garlic in a saucepan. Add the white wine and bring to a boil, lower the heat and reduce the liquid by two thirds. Add the lemon juice and chicken stock and reduce again by half. Add the cream, bring to a boil and then remove from the heat. Strain the sauce through a fine sieve pressing on the garlic. Add the chopped rosemary and season with salt and pepper and let simmer while carving the lamb.

Carve the lamb between the bones. Place three chops on each warmed dinner plate. Drizzle over and around the garlic cream and serve with the roasted root vegetables. Garnish with a sprig of fresh rosemary.

LEGUMES ROTIS
Roasted Root Vegetables

All root vegetables contain sugars that caramelize when they are roasted, imparting a concentrated earthiness as well as natural sweetness. Here that sweetness balances the tanginess of the lemon and garlic cream.

4 tablespoons canola or sunflower oil
2 tablespoons unsalted butter
2 pounds mixed root vegetables (such as turnip, rutabaga, celery root, carrot,

Jerusalem artichoke) all cut into 2-inch chunks
Fine sea salt
Freshly ground black pepper

Preheat the oven to 375°F.

Heat the oil and butter in a large roasting pan on top of the stove. Put in the vegetables and stir-fry for 5 minutes over a high heat, until well colored. Season and add just enough water to half cover the vegetables. Bring to a boil and reduce the liquid by half. Transfer to the oven and cook for 20 minutes until the water has evaporated and the vegetables are tender. Give a stir and continue cooking for another 10 minutes until the vegetables are well-colored. Season and keep warm; or let cool and reheat them later when needed.

> WINE
>
> This is, at the same time, a hearty, earthy roast, but one made with quality ingredients and garnished with finesse. That calls for a wine with similar credentials. A nice Nuit-St Georges or a village Gevrey-Chambertin would give you the rustic earthiness, yet there is no denying the pedigree.

CREPINETTES D'AGNEAU AU FROMAGE DE CHEVRE
Bacon Wrapped Lamb Noisettes with Goat Cheese
6 Servings

These lamb 'packets' can be assembled ahead of time and roasted for 20 minutes just before serving.

I serve them very simply, on a green salad with lightly toasted almonds.

The goats' cheese that I use in this recipe are little *Crottin de Chavignol*, from the Loire valley near Sancerre. They are shaped in small rounds, about 2-inches across and an inch tall. You don't want them too fresh nor too old and shrunken. They should still be moist and creamy, but hold together when baked.

12 loin-cut lamb noisettes cut one-inch thick	For the salad:
Fine seal salt	1 large bowl mixed salad greens
Freshly ground black pepper	½ cup skinned lightly toasted almonds
2 tablespoons Dijon mustard	2 shallots thinly sliced
12 large pitted prunes or six small fresh figs cut in two	3 teaspoons sherry vinegar
6 sheets phyllo dough (found in the frozen section of most supermarkets)	6 tablespoons canola oil
6 small goat cheese rounds, sliced in half to make 12 slices	Fine sea salt
4 tablespoons melted unsalted butter	Freshly ground black pepper

In a heavy sauté pan, sear the lamb noisettes for a minute on each side over a brisk heat in a little oil and butter. Let them cool. Season the noisettes with salt and pepper then smear each with mustard. Thaw the phyllo according to packet directions and brush one phyllo sheet with melted butter (keep the remaining sheets well covered so they don't dry out) and cut into a strip approximately 6-inches wide. Place a seared noisette on the end of one strip. Top the lamb with a slice of goat cheese, top this with a prune or fig half and season with salt and pepper, and fold as neatly as possible, making a package. Do all the noisettes this way and reserve on a baking tray.

Preheat the oven to 375°F.

Roast the packets in the preheated oven for 20 minutes until golden brown.

Make the vinaigrette by dissolving a teaspoon of sea salt in the sherry vinegar. Add the sliced shallots and let them macerate in the vinegar to soften their flavor while the lamb is cooking.

Just before serving whisk in the oil and black pepper into the shallot mixture. Toss with the greens and almonds. Divide the salad among six plates. Top with two lamb chops per person and serve.

WINE

This is an earthy dish, but light at the same time. So we look for a wine keeping with that profile: a Pinot from the fringes. A St. Aubin red or a fairly rare red Meursault would give you plenty of fruit, but with the rustic edge you're looking for. Another possibility: a village Nuits-St. Georges would work well too; slightly 'animal'; gutsy, but fruity.

FILET DE BICHE AU CASSIS ET GRATIN DE CHOUFLEUR AU GINGEMBRE
Venison Filet with Blackcurrants and a Ginger Cauliflower Gratin
6 Servings

Biche is doe, a deer, a female deer. (It is also a French term of endearment, as is 'dear' in English.) If you like your meat well done, filet of venison is not for you. Cooked beyond medium rare, it becomes savorless and dry. If, on the other hand, you like your meat fairly rare, deer meat can be very elegant; dense, dark and tender, with little fat.

The leg, haunch and saddle are the choicest joints. The filet that is prepared here is the best of all. There is no need to marinate a filet, especially if it is from a young doe. The color of what little fat there is can be an indication of age: young animal fat is white, while an older animal's is yellow.

This sauce can also be made with cooking cherries using exactly the same quantities, just replacing the currants with the cherries. Both sauces would go well with other types of game such as duck or wild boar.

Serve the venison with the cauliflower gratin below or other autumnal vegetables such as pumpkin, brussel sprouts or turnips.

For the sauce:
2 tablespoons sugar
I cup red wine
4 tablespoons red wine vinegar
2 cups blackcurrants preferably fresh, or frozen rather than jarred
I tablespoon cornstarch
2 tablespoons unsalted butter
Fine sea salt

Freshly ground black pepper
¾ cup of veal or chicken stock

For the meat:
12–18 medallions of deer cut ½-inch thick from the filet
I tablespoon unsalted butter
I tablespoon cooking oil
Fine sea salt
Freshly ground black pepper

Bring the wine, sugar and vinegar to a boil. Reduce the heat and cook for 20 minutes. Add the cassis berries and cook for a further 10 minutes. Mix the cornstarch with 3 tablespoons of cold water to form a thin paste. Stir this into the sauce and reserve.

In a heavy-bottomed sauté pan, melt the butter with the oil. When the foaming has subsided, add the deer medallions and cook 3–4 minutes on each side to no more than medium rare. Do not overcrowd the pan (the meat will steam instead of sautéing). Better to do the sauté in batches, removing the pieces to a warm platter as you go. Season the filets with salt and pepper and keep them warm while you finish the sauce. Pour off any fat and add the stock to the pan. Let it reduce to a ¼ cup and then add the blackcurrant sauce. Let it bubble to the desired consistency (where it lightly naps a spoon). Taste the sauce for seasoning and swirl in the remaining 2 tablespoons of butter. When the butter is incorporated, remove the pan from the heat and return the medallions to the sauce to re-heat.

GRATIN DE CHOUFLEUR AU GINGEMBRE
Cauliflower and Ginger Gratin

I cauliflower	Freshly ground black pepper
Juice of a half lemon	2 cups heavy cream
Fine sea salt	2 inches peeled fresh ginger grated

Preheat the oven to 375°F.

Bring a large pot of salted water to a boil. Wash the cauliflower and break into small flowerets. When the water comes to a boil add the lemon juice and the cauliflower. Cook for 5 minutes, drain and refresh under cold water until cool.

Put the cream in a saucepan with the grated ginger, bring to boil, reduce to a simmer and cook until reduced by half. Strain through a fine sieve. Season the cream with salt and pepper to taste. Put the cauliflower in a gratin plate, pour over the cream and bake for 20 minutes, until browned and bubbly.

> WINE
>
> Traditionally, everyone says that you should save your big-gun wines for game. And here you could follow the maxim with success. Think older Aloxe-Corton premier cru or Gevrey Chambertin from one of the great vineyards.

DAUBE DE SANGLIER ET POMMES DE TERRE RAPÉES
Wild Boar in Red Wine with a Burgundian Potato Galette
6 Servings

You will have to do some advance planning for this recipe as the wild boar benefits from a marinade for a day or two to tenderize the meat before cooking. A meaty leg of venison also works well in this type of preparation.

Here at home, we never have a problem deciding what wine to use for these slow-cooked stewy dishes. It's a funny story. When we first arrived in Burgundy, we found recipes in the old cookbooks for things like 'Coq au Chambertin'. We'd laugh: 'coq au vin', ok; but who would use 'grand cru' wine for a stew? Well, one day we were tasting with Jean Raphet in Morey-St. Denis. He and his wife like their food, so we were talking about cooking, and Madame Raphet asked me if I wanted some Charmes-Chambertin lees. Well, the little light came on. She was asking if I wanted the bottled sediment of a 'grand cru' wine! Up she comes from the cellar with these crusty old bottles of well-aged (she said it had to be well-aged) Chambertin lees. And ever since we've always had a little stash in the cellar of the best cooking wine you've ever tasted.

You could serve this *daube* with plain steamed potatoes, polenta or pasta. I like to serve it with these potato and cheese pancakes to soak up all the delicious sauce.

4 pounds wild boar meat from the shoulder and/or leg
2 onions
1 carrot
3 garlic cloves
1 *bouquet garni* made of bay leaf, parsley and thyme
4 cloves

2 one-inch strips of orange zest
10 peppercorns
1 bottle red wine
3 tablespoons red wine vinegar
3 tablespoons olive oil
3 tablespoons unsalted butter
Fine sea salt
Freshly ground black pepper

For the thickening agent, a *beurre manie:*
2 tablespoons unsalted butter at room temperature and 2 tablespoons all purpose flour.

Cut the meat into two-inch cubed chunks. Put the meat in a large bowl. Coarsely chop the onion and carrot, lightly crush the garlic cloves and add them to the bowl. Make the *bouquet garni* by tying up 2 bay leaves, a handful of parsley sprigs and a large branch of thyme with kitchen twine. Add this to the bowl along with the cloves, orange peel, peppercorns, wine and red wine vinegar. Stir the mixture and add some water if the meat is not entirely covered by the marinade. Drizzle over a little olive oil, cover and refrigerate 24–48 hours, stirring the mixture once or twice in that time.

Preheat the oven to 300°F.

Lift the meat from the marinade with a slotted spoon and pat the meat dry with paper towel. Strain the marinade, reserving the liquid and the vegetables. In a large heavy-bottom casserole or Dutch oven, heat the oil and butter over high heat until foaming. Add a few pieces of meat to the hot fat and brown well on all sides. Don't add too much meat to the pan at once. You want the meat to sear, so work in batches. Once all the meat has been browned and removed from the pan, add the reserved vegetables (not the *bouquet garni*) from the marinade and, over medium heat, cook them until lightly browned, about 5–8 minutes. Add the marinade liquid slowly and bring it to a boil. Let it boil for a couple of minutes to cook off the alcohol and then add the browned beef to the liquid. Push the meat down into the liquid and add the *bouquet garni*. Wet a piece of parchment paper that is roughly the size of the pan and place on top of the meat. Cover the pot and put it into the preheated oven. After 30 minutes check the meat to make sure that it is cooking at a low simmer. Return to the oven and continue to cook for and additional 1½ to 2 hours until very tender when pronged with a fork.

For the *beurre manie*: Knead the butter and flour together in a small bowl. Chill.

When the boar is tender, remove it from the oven. Lift out the chunks with a slotted spoon and set aside. Strain the sauce through a fine strainer, pressing well to extract all of the flavor from the vegetables. Pour the sauce back into the pan and bring it to a boil. Whisk in the *beurre manie* 1 teaspoon at a time into the bubbling sauce. When all the lumps have dissolved, season the sauce to taste and reduce until your sauce naps a spoon nicely. Return the meat to the sauce and at this point, you can cool the daube, and reheat it when ready to serve. It will taste even better the next day. Serve hot from the casserole, if you like.

POMMES DE TERRE RAPÉ
Potato and Cheese Pancakes

Here in Burgundy I use local *fromage blanc*, or fresh farmers' cheese, for these pancakes. If *fromage blanc* is not available, substitute *ricotta* cheese.

I pound waxy potatoes, such as Yukon gold
I tablespoon all purpose flour
I large egg
Unsalted butter
Canola oil

¾ cup *fromage blanc* or *ricotta* cheese
3 tablespoons chopped chives
Fine sea salt
Freshly ground black pepper

Peel the potatoes and grate them in a food processor or with a fine hand grater. Put the grated potato into a bowl and mix immediately with the other ingredients.

In a large non-stick sauté pan, heat a tablespoon of butter with a little canola oil over medium heat. With a large spoon drop in the potato mixture and let the pancakes cook and brown lightly on one side. Flip the pancakes and brown the other side. Remove the pancakes to a platter, season with salt and pepper and keep warm while making the rest. Serve the pancakes warm.

> WINE
>
> The gaminess of the wild boar calls for a gutsy red. In Burgundy this will be an aged, noble wine from the Cotes de Nuits. Think big!

DESSERTS

CROUSTILLANT DE FRAMBOISES A LA CRÈME D'ORANGE
Glazed Almond Phyllo with Raspberries and Orange Cream

POIRES ET FIGUES POCHÉES AU BOUILLON DE CANNELLE
GLACE AU MIEL D'ACACIA
Pears and Figs in a Cinnamon Bouillon with Acacia Honey Ice Cream

GLACE AUX PRUNEAUX ET AU MARC DE BOURGOGNE
Prune Ice Cream with Marc de Bourgogne

MELON CHAUD AU POIVRE BLANC ET GLACE AU CHOCOLAT
BLANC
Warm Melon with White Pepper and White Chocolate Ice Cream

TARTE TATIN AUX COINGS ET SORBET A L'ESTRAGON
Caramelized Quince Tart with Tarragon Sorbet

SOUFFLE AU CITRON
Lemon Soufflé

CRÈME LEGERE AU CHOCOLAT ET AUX CHÂTAIGNES
A Light Chocolate and Chestnut Mousse

GATEAU ROULÉ A LA MOUSSE AU CHOCOLAT ET AU GINGEMBRE
Rolled Chocolate Cake with a Chocolate and Ginger Filling

TARTE AU CASSIS
Black Currant Tart

SORBET CASSIS ET MERINGUE
Cassis Sorbet with Meringue

GATEAU DE PISTACHES AUX ABRICOTS FRAIS
Fresh Apricot and Pistachio Cake

GLACE AU CITRON ET AU BASILIC
Lemon and Basil Ice Cream

SOUPE AUX PECHES DE VIGNE A L'IRANCY
Warm Vine Peach Soup with Irancy Wine

PAIN D'ÉPICES
Burgundian Spice Bread

PAIN D'ÉPICES PERDU AUX POIRES
Spice Bread Pudding with Pear

GLACE DE PAIN D'ÉPICES AUX POIRES CARAMELISÉES
Spice Bread Ice Cream with Caramelized Pears

PARFAIT DE RHUBARBE À LA FRAISE
Rhubarb and Strawberry Parfait

CROUSTILLANT DE FRAMBOISES A LA CRÈME D'ORANGE
Glazed Almond Phyllo with Raspberries and Orange Cream
6 Servings

Everything here can be made ahead of time and assembled just before serving. It's a striking dessert, as beautiful to look at as it is to eat. The orange cream is lighter than regular pastry cream. It would make a wonderful filling also for a fresh fruit tart like the Blackcurrant Tart in this section.

For the layered phyllo rectangles:
4 sheets phyllo dough
4 tablespoons unsalted butter melted
½ cup fine granulated sugar mixed with the zest of one lemon
1 cup sliced or slivered almonds, lightly toasted

4 cups fresh raspberries
4 tablespoons fine granulated sugar
1 teaspoon lemon juice

For the pastry cream:
1 cup milk scalded with one split vanilla bean
3 large egg yolks
½ cup granulated sugar
2 scant tablespoons cornstarch
Juice of half an orange
2 tablespoon Cointreau or Grand Marnier
½ cup heavy cream well chilled

Preheat the oven to 375°F.

For the phyllo rectangles: Lay down one sheet of phyllo on a cutting board. Brush with the melted butter; sprinkle with 1/3 of the lemon sugar, and 1/3 of the toasted almonds. Repeat this process twice ending with a sheet of phyllo. Brush the last sheet with melted butter. Then with a very sharp knife, cut the phyllo rectangle into three even strips lengthwise. Cut each strip into 6 even pieces. Place them on a heavy baking sheet, cover with a piece of parchment paper, and place another baking sheet on top to weight them down. Bake for ten minutes, then remove the top tray and the paper. Put the rectangles back in the oven for approximately five minutes longer until nicely browned. Remove, let cool and reserve.

For the raspberry *coulis*: Crush 2 cups of the raspberries in a bowl with a fork. Add the sugar and lemon juice. Set aside for a half-hour and then strain through a fine sieve pressing hard on the fruit. Cover and refrigerate until needed.

For the pastry cream: Scald the milk and the split vanilla bean (try to scrape out as many seeds with your knife as you can from the bean, adding them to the milk as well). Beat the egg yolks and sugar in a bowl until pale-lemon colored. Whisk in the cornstarch. Remove the vanilla bean from the scalded milk and whisk the milk into the egg yolk mixture. Pour the mixture back into the pan and heat over a low fire, whisking all the while, until the mixture thickens and starts to bubble. Cook for 2 minutes more; and then immediately scrape the mixture into a clean bowl to cool. Once cool, whisk in the orange juice and add the Cointreau. Beat the heavy cream in a separate bowl until thick and fluffy, and gently whisk this into the orange cream. Cover and refrigerate.

To assemble: On six individual serving plates, place a rectangle off-center on the plate. Top with a tablespoon of the orange filling and a few berries. Cover this with another rectangle pressing down gently to hold it in place. Top with another tablespoon of cream, more berries and drizzle over two tablespoons of *coulis*. Finish with another rectangle, drizzle around another tablespoon of *coulis* and garnish with any remaining raspberries and a sprig of mint.

POIRES ET FIGUES POCHÉES AU BOUILLON DE CANNELLE GLACE AU MIEL D'ACACIA

Pears and Figs in a Cinnamon Bouillon with Acacia Honey Ice Cream
6 Servings

Of all the honeys that I have tasted, Acacia is my favorite. I look for a clear, runny honey with a light, clean taste. Acacia blossoms also make delicious fritters, dipped in batter, deep fried and then dusted with sugar.

This is a perfect autumnal dessert, warm and soothing. You could make this ahead of time and gently reheat when ready to serve.

6 large firm fresh black figs
3 large firm but ripe pears
4 tablespoons unsalted butter
½ cup granulated sugar
2 cinnamon sticks about 2-inches in length each

¾ cup water
I quart honey ice cream
(see recipe below)
Mint for garnish

Peel the pears, quarter and core them. Slice each quarter into 3 even slices. Quarter the figs. Melt the butter in a large sauté pan with lid. Add the sugar and the pear slices and toss to coat. Add the water and the cinnamon sticks. Bring to a boil and reduce heat to its lowest setting, cover the pan and simmer for 5 minutes. Add the figs at this point. Cover and simmer for an additional 10 minutes. In large shallow soup bowls place 5 slices of pear with a fig quarter between each slice. Put a scoop or two of ice cream in the bowl and spoon over a couple of tablespoons of the cinnamon bouillon. Serve immediately.

For the Acacia Honey Ice Cream:
2 cups heavy cream
I cup milk
½ cup of acacia or lavender honey

In a saucepan combine the cream, milk and honey. Bring to a simmer over a low fire and remove from the heat. Let cool completely, then freeze in an ice cream machine.

GLACE AUX PRUNEAUX ET AU MARC DE BOURGOGNE
Prune Ice Cream with Marc de Bourgogne
8–10 Servings

While this delicious ice cream needs a good bit of forethought, it's worth the time and effort. The prunes need to be marinated in the alcohol syrup for a week in advance to give the ice cream the desired richness. After that, it's easy. You can substitute the *Marc de Bourgogne* with Armagnac or Cognac with equal success.

For the syrup:
¾ cup granulated sugar
¾ cup water
¾ cup *Marc de Bourgogne*
24 large pitted prunes

For the ice cream:
1 cup milk
1 vanilla pod split or a teaspoon of vanilla extract
2 egg yolks
½ cup granulated sugar
2 cups chilled heavy cream

At least 5 days ahead, you must macerate the prunes in the *marc* syrup. Bring the sugar, *marc*, and water to a boil in a small saucepan and boil for 5 minutes. Let cool and pour this over 24 large pitted prunes. Cover and refrigerate.

To make the ice cream: Scald 1 cup of milk with the split vanilla bean. In a bowl, beat the 2 yolks with the ½ cup of sugar until pale and thick. Add the scalded milk slowly in a stream, whisking all the time. Return this mixture to the pan and place over a medium low heat, stirring with a wooden spoon until it thickens slightly. Remove from heat and pour the mixture into a cool bowl. When completely cool, add the cold cream and put the mixture into an ice cream maker to freeze.

Chop 12 of the prunes finely. Mix the chopped prunes with 1/3 cup of the Marc syrup. Add this to the ice cream when the ice cream is almost frozen. Continue to freeze until firm. Reserve frozen. Serve the ice cream with the remaining whole prunes and drizzle over some of the syrup.

> WINE
>
> *Marc de Bourgogne* is the Burgundian version of *grappa*: it's the grape skins—and in the case of a *'fine de Bourgogne'*, the last pressing of the grapes—distilled and aged. While most *grappa* is clear; *marc* is amber like cognac. This is because it is aged in oak, and takes on the color and flavor of the barrel. As with *grappa*, there are many levels of quality. You don't want to buy a cheap one!

MELON CHAUD AU POIVRE BLANC ET GLACE AU CHOCOLAT BLANC
Warm Melon with White Pepper and White Chocolate Ice Cream
10 Servings

This recipe is based on one from Dijon chef Jean-Paul Thibert. It's very simple to make and the combination of the warm melon and white pepper with the white chocolate ice cream works really well.

Make sure that the melons you use for this recipe are sweet and ripe, yet still firm. It is also important to use freshly ground white pepper.

2 large firm cantaloupes
Freshly ground white pepper

For the ice cream:
2 cups whole milk
7 oz. good quality white chocolate

For the layered phyllo crisps:
4 sheets phyllo dough
2 tablespoon unsalted butter melted
¼ cup finely granulated sugar

Bring the milk to a simmer in a saucepan. Remove from the heat and add the chocolate broken into pieces. Let sit 5 minutes, then whisk the mixture smooth. Strain through a fine sieve and chill. Whisk again when cool and put the mixture in an ice cream maker and freeze.

Preheat the oven to 375°F.

Lay down on sheet of phyllo on a cutting board. Brush with the melted butter; sprinkle with the sugar and top with the remaining phyllo sheet. Brush again with butter. Then with a very sharp knife, cut the phyllo rectangle into 2 even strips lengthwise. Cut each strip into 5 even pieces. Place them on a heavy baking sheet, cover with a piece of parchment paper, and place another baking sheet on top to weight them down. Bake for ten minutes, then remove the top tray and the paper. Put the crisps back in the oven until lightly golden brown. Remove, let cool and reserve. Repeat this process with the 2 remaining phyllo sheets. You should have 20 crisps in all.

Cut the melons in half. Scrap out the seeds and, using a large melon baller, scoop out the flesh into neat rounds. Heat a large heavy-bottomed non-stick sauté pan over a medium heat. When warm, put in the melon pieces and heat through, grinding over the white pepper. Put the warm melon in shallow bowls placing quite a few tightly together in the center of each bowl leaving some melon out towards the edges. Balance a phyllo crisp on top of the melon in the center of each bowl, top with a scoop of the ice cream and gently wedge a phyllo crisp like a sail into the top of each scoop of ice cream. Serve immediately.

TARTE TATIN AUX COINGS ET SORBET A L'ESTRAGON
Caramelized Quince Tart with Tarragon Sorbet
10–12 Servings

This is a classic Tarte Tatin, but made with quince in place of apple. But it is really the tarragon sorbet that makes this recipe special. The sorbet itself takes minutes to make, and it is a taste that plays off the tart perfectly.

Tarte Tatin can easily end up a runny mess. But follow this recipe closely and you should be able to flip out a beauty.

Use a 12 inch glass pie dish if you can; it will allow you to check the color of the caramel as the tart bakes

For the shortcrust:
1 cup all-purpose flour
Pinch granulated sugar
8 tablespoons (1 stick) cold unsalted butter
Pinch of salt
2 tablespoons cold water

For the caramel:
1 cup granulated sugar
½ cup water
A few drops of lemon juice

For the quince:
6 quinces peeled, quartered removing the centers

For the pastry: place the flour, butter (cut into pieces), sugar, and salt into the bowl of a food processor. Process, pulsing, for about 45 seconds, until the butter is incorporated. Add the water; process again until the dough starts to form a ball. Stop; gather up the pastry; form it into a ball and refrigerate.

Preheat the oven to 375°F.

Butter a glass pie dish.

Make the caramel by dissolving the sugar with the water and lemon juice in a small saucepan. Once the sugar has dissolved, do not stir the syrup again. Cook for 15–20 minutes until you have a light-tan colored caramel. Pour immediately into the buttered glass pie plate and tilt the dish to coat it as well as possible. *Be very careful with the caramel, it is extremely hot!*

Put the quince quarters into a saucepan and cover with water and add a pinch of cinnamon. Bring to a boil and cook over a low fire for 10 minutes. Remove them from the liquid with a slotted spoon and let drain. Place the pieces of quince on the caramel rounded sides facing down as tightly as possible. Put the quince in the oven and bake for 20 minutes until they have started to absorb the caramel. Remove from the oven.

Roll out the pastry to a 1/3-inch-thick round, large enough to cover the pie dish. If the dough is too firm, bang the dough ball repeatedly with the rolling pin to warm it a bit. Place the pastry gently on top of the quince. Pierce with a knife in 4 or 5 places. Put the tart on a baking sheet (because the juices often bubble over). Bake 50 minutes. When you remove the tart from the oven, check that the caramel is a rich, brown color. If it is still pale, put it back in the oven. If the pastry browns too quickly, cover it with foil. Bake until the caramel is ready. Remove from the oven; wait 15 minutes before flipping out onto a platter. Serve each slice with a scoop of tarragon sorbet.

SORBET A L'ESTRAGON
Tarragon Sorbet

2 cups full fat milk
½ cup granulated sugar

2 tablespoons fresh tarragon minced
2 teaspoon heavy cream

In a saucepan, bring the milk, sugar, and cream to a boil. Add the tarragon and simmer for 5 minutes. Let cool completely and freeze in an ice cream maker. Best served on the day you make it.

SOUFFLE AU CITRON
Lemon Soufflé
Makes 8 individual soufflés

This very light and very lemony soufflé is an impressive sight. Baked in a shallow water bath (which accounts for its texture creamy), it rises 2 to 3 inches above the mold, forming a golden crust when done. Avoid the temptation to open the oven door and peek. A constant temperature is most important. If you have an oven light and a glass door, you are in luck.

As with any soufflé, it is essential that the eggs be as fresh as possible and at room temperature when you start.

You will need 8 3-inch tall soufflé molds with a 1½ cup capacity each.

For the soufflé:
8 large fresh eggs separated
2 extra egg whites
½ cup granulated sugar for the soufflé base
The zest and juice of 2–3 lemons, depending on their size and juiciness

¼ cup granulated sugar for mounting the egg whites
A pinch of salt
3 tablespoons softened unsalted butter for the soufflé molds
¼ cup sugar for the molds

Preheat the oven to 425°F and place an oven rack slightly higher than halfway up in the oven.

Butter the soufflé molds evenly. Coat the inside of the molds with the quarter cup of sugar, one at a time, tipping out the excess sugar into the next mold etc. Discard any excess sugar at the end.

Whisk the egg yolks for 3 minutes. Add the ½ cup of sugar slowly and continue whisking until the mixture is pale yellow. Stir in the lemon zest and ½ cup of the lemon juice. Add a pinch of salt to the egg whites and whisk to soft peaks. Add the remaining ¼ cup of sugar and whisk until glossy but not grainy. Gently fold 1/3 of the whites into the yolk mixture and then gently fold in the remaining whites. Spoon the mixture into the prepared molds right to the top. Scrape the surface flat with a spatula. Run the tip of your thumb around the inside rim of the molds to form a shallow trough against the edge. This will allow the soufflé to rise evenly and freely.

Place the molds in a shallow baking tray. Pour in hot water around the outside bottoms of the molds to a depth of ¼ of an inch. Bake in the oven for 10–12 minutes until risen and browned. Serve immediately.

CRÈME LEGERE AU CHOCOLAT ET AUX CHÂTAIGNES
A Light Chocolate and Chestnut Mousse
10 Servings

Look for unsweetened chestnut puree, but if you can't find it, it's easy to make. Simply purée vacuum-packed or jarred, peeled chestnuts. I serve this mousse topped with quality candied orange peel and a small glass of Grand Marnier A perfect simple wintertime dessert.

½ cup granulated sugar
½ cup water
7 ounces bittersweet or semi-sweet dark chocolate such as Lindt 70% cocoa

1 teaspoon vanilla extract
2 cups pureed chestnut
1½ cups heavy cream chilled
Strips of candied orange peel to garnish

In a small saucepan, boil the sugar and water together until a light syrup forms. Approximately 4–5 minutes. Break the chocolate into pieces and let melt in the warm syrup. Let cool slightly and add the vanilla. Stir in the pureed chestnut and let cool completely.

In a chilled bowl beat the cream until thick and light. Save a quarter cup of the whipped cream for garnishing the mousses. Gently fold the rest of the cream into the chestnut mixture and incorporate well. Spoon the mixture into decorative serving glasses and chill the mixture for 2 hours. Serve with a dollop of cream and a few strips of candied orange peel.

GATEAU ROULÉ A LA MOUSSE AU CHOCOLAT ET AU GINGEMBRE
Rolled Chocolate Cake with a Chocolate and Ginger Filling
10–12 Servings

Serve this very-chocolate dessert with a fresh mango coulis. Beautiful colors, and a delicious flavor combination.

You can present this cake as a roulade as described here; or alternatively as a layer cake: cut the cake into three separate pieces, spreading the mousse on two and topping with the third piece.

You will need an oblong baking tray, 8 x 14 inches and 1 inch deep, lightly oiled and the base lined with parchment paper.

Pre-heat the oven to 350°F.

For the Chocolate Cake:
6 large eggs separated
$^2/_3$ cup caster or finely granulated sugar
2 ounces unsweetened cocoa powder
Confectioners' sugar for dusting

For the Chocolate Mousse:
2 teaspoon peeled and freshly grated ginger
1 cup heavy cream

10 ounces dark semi-sweet or bittersweet chocolate such as Lindt 70% cocoa
3 tablespoons unsalted butter, softened to room temperature
2 egg whites
$^1/_4$ cup caster or finely granulated sugar
Pinch of salt

Start by making the cake. Separate the eggs and in a large bowl whisk the yolks with the caster sugar until pale and slightly thickened. Mix in the cocoa powder. In another large clean bowl beat the egg whites to the soft-peak stage. Gently and thoroughly fold the whites into the cocoa mixture, then pour the mixture into the prepared baking tray.

Bake the cake on the center shelf until puffed and springy 12–15 minutes. Remove from the oven and leave to cool in the pan. When completely cool, turn it out on to an oblong sheet of parchment paper that has been liberally dusted with confectioners' sugar. Peel away the parchment paper from the bottom of the cake.

Make the mousse by heating in a small pan ½ cup of heavy cream with the grated ginger. Let steep for 15 minutes and then strain out the ginger using a fine sieve. Return the ½ cup of cream to the pan and heat again. Break the chocolate into pieces and off the fire add the chocolate to the warm cream. Let the chocolate melt into the cream and then add the butter. You may need to put the chocolate pan into another larger pan with very hot water in order to melt it. When the mixture is smooth let cool, stirring from time to time.

In a large chilled bowl, beat the remaining ½ cup of chilled cream to soft peaks. In another bowl beat the egg white with the salt. When soft peaks form add the sugar and continue to beat for a minute or two until fairly stiff. Gently fold the egg whites into the cream. Fold 1/3 of the chocolate mixture into the cream thoroughly and then gently fold in the rest of the chocolate until well blended.

Spread the chocolate mousse filling over the cake and then gently roll the cake to make a log shape. Cover lightly with a foil tent and chill for an hour or more. Serve the cake in thin slices on a plate with the mango coulis on the side.

TARTE AU CASSIS
Black Currant Tart
8–10 Servings

Black currant or 'cassis' has a long association with Burgundian cooking. Perhaps because of the link with *kir*, the white wine and *cassis* aperitif that is drunk everywhere in Burgundy; perhaps because the region seems to be its natural habitat: the plant thrives. You'll find it in menus from starters right through to desserts. When we were living in our Burgundy Canal lock house, we had two gorgeous bushes in the garden. They took no care, little pruning, and supplied us with more *cassis* that we could use in the season. We now always have a sack or two of berries in the freezer to provide a little taste of summer freshness in the middle of the Burgundian winter.

Pate Sucrée for one 10-inch tart:
1 cup unbleached all-purpose flour
1 stick cold unsalted butter cubed
2 tablespoons sugar
Pinch of salt
3 tablespoons of cold water

For the pastry cream:
1 cup milk scalded with one split vanilla bean
3 large egg yolks
½ cup granulated sugar
3 scant tablespoons cornstarch

Juice of half an orange
2 tablespoon Cointreau or Grand Marnier
½ cup heavy cream well chilled

Cassis topping:
1 cup granulated sugar
3 tablespoons cornstarch
1 cup water
¼ teaspoon salt
1 tablespoon unsalted butter
4 cups of fresh or frozen cassis berries

For the pastry cream: Scald the milk and the split vanilla bean (try to scrape out as many seeds with your knife as you can from the bean adding them to the milk as well). Beat the egg yolks and sugar in a bowl until pale-lemon colored. Whisk in the cornstarch. Remove the vanilla bean from the scalded milk and whisk the milk into the egg yolk mixture. Pour the mixture back into the pan and heat over a low fire, whisking all the while, until the mixture thickens and starts to bubble. Cook for 2 minutes more; then immediately scrape the mixture into a clean bowl to cool. Once cool, whisk in the orange juice and add the Cointreau. Beat the heavy cream in a separate bowl until thick and fluffy and then gently whisk this into the orange cream. Cover and refrigerate

Make the pastry by combining the flour, butter, sugar and salt in the bowl of a food processor. Combine until the butter is incorporated (a minute or so). Stop the machine and add the cold water. Pulse just until the mixture starts to come together, but stop before it forms a ball. Remove the pastry, pat into a ball, wrap in wax paper and refrigerate 20 to 30 minutes to allow it to firm up.

Flour a work surface and roll out the dough. Line a 10- or 12-inch fluted tart pan with removable bottom with the dough, trim the excess and prick the bottom with a fork. Refrigerate for at least an hour before baking.

Preheat the oven to 400°F.

Line the tart shell with foil or parchment paper and fill with dried beans or rice to weight it down. Bake in the middle of the oven for 15 minutes. Remove the paper and beans and return the pastry to the oven for an additional 15 minutes until golden. Let cool completely.

For the *cassis* topping: Mix the sugar, cornstarch, water and salt in a saucepan. Whisking, bring the mixture to a boil and let thicken. Add the cassis berries and cook slowly for another 4 minutes. Remove from the heat and add the butter. Let cool completely stirring from time to time.

Fill the cooled pastry shell with the orange cream and top with the cassis berries. Serve chilled or at room temperature.

SORBET CASSIS ET MERINGUE
Cassis Sorbet with Meringue
10 Servings

We had this wonderful dessert in a restaurant near Dijon's lively covered market. *Le Bistro des Halles* is the smaller, simpler restaurant of Dijon's Michelin-chef Jean-Pierre Billoux. These off-shoot restaurants have become very popular with many of the big-name chefs. It's a great opportunity to eat imaginative food in a casual setting at reasonable prices.

If Dijon is on your itinerary, try to make it on market days, Tuesday, Friday and Saturday. It's one of the great city markets, set in and around a market hall designed by Eiffel; not to be missed.

For the meringues:
4 large egg whites at room temperature
1¼ cups granulated sugar
2 teaspoons cornstarch
Splash of white wine vinegar

For the simple syrup:
1½ cups granulated sugar
1¾ cups water

For the sorbet:
1¼ pounds black currant berries to obtain 1¼ cups of sieved juice. Reserve 1 cup of whole berries for the sauce.
Juice of a half lemon
1 teaspoon of egg white beaten frothy with a fork

For the sauce:
1 cup reserved cassis berries
½ cup granulated sugar
4 tablespoons *crème de cassis*

Preheat the oven to 200°F. Cover a cookie sheet with parchment paper.

Beat the whites (preferably in a large copper bowl) until they are firm, then add ¾ of the sugar and beat for a minute more until shiny. Stop and sprinkle over the remaining sugar, cornstarch and vinegar. Continue beating for another two minutes. Using a large sauce spoon put ten mounds of meringue on the parchment paper. With the back of the spoon make a shallow indentation in each mound, deep enough to hold a scoop of sorbet. Bake for 1 to 1½ hours until the meringues are dry but not colored. The trick is to cook them slowly. When done, they should lift off the parchment paper easily. Let them cool in the off-oven with the door closed for a couple of hours.

Make the syrup by putting the sugar and water in a saucepan and bring to a boil. Reduce by a third and let the syrup cool. Chill.

Puree the blackcurrants in a food processor with the juice of a half lemon. Strain the puree through a fine sieve, pressing on the solids to obtain 11/3 cups of juice. Mix the cassis juice with the chilled syrup and put this mixture in an ice cream machine. When the mixture is almost frozen, add the small amount of lightly beaten egg white and continue processing for a couple of minutes. You will notice immediately that the sorbet will begin to become fluffier. It's the egg white at the end that gives the sorbet it silky texture.

In a small saucepan, heat the remaining cup of cassis berries with the ½ cup of sugar. Bring to a boil and simmer just until the berries start to pop. Add the crème de cassis, let cool and reserve.

Serve in shallow bowls topping each meringue case with a scoop of sorbet and spooning some of the sauce over and around each one.

GATEAU DE PISTACHES AUX ABRICOTS FRAIS
Fresh Apricot and Pistachio Cake
10–12 Servings

I love the combination of fresh apricot and raw green pistachio nuts. I often serve warm sautéed apricots with a scoop of pistachio ice cream for a quick simple dessert. In this recipe the nuts are coarsely chopped to line the baking pan and top the cake for a crunchy texture. The apricots melt into the cake batter when baked and remain juicy and delicious. And the color combination is beautiful.

1½ pounds fresh apricots washed and split in half, pit removed
1 cup raw peeled green pistachio nuts
¾ cup granulated sugar
2 sticks unsalted butter softened to room temperature

4 large eggs
1 teaspoon vanilla extract
½ teaspoon fine salt
1 cup all purpose flour mixed with
1 teaspoon baking powder.

A 12 inch buttered cake pan.

Preheat the oven to 375°F.

If you need to skin the pistachio nuts, blanch them in boiling water for 5 minutes. Remove and rub the nuts in a kitchen cloth to remove the skins. Add the nuts to a processor and pulse chop for a coarse grind. Remove half the nuts and then continue processing the other nuts until you have a fine grind.

Sprinkle half the coarsely chopped nuts into the bottom of the buttered cake pan. Reserve the other half of the coarsely chopped nuts for the top of the cake.

In a bowl beat the softened butter and sugar together until creamed. Add the eggs one at a time beating well after each addition and then add the finely ground nuts. Add the vanilla, salt and then the flour mixed with baking powder.

Pour the batter into the buttered cake pan. Cut each apricot half in half and arrange the cut apricots skin side down in the batter. Sprinkle lightly with sugar and the remaining coarsely chopped nuts. Bake for 45–50 minutes until lightly browned and slightly puffed. Serve warm or at room temperature with some *cream fraîche* if you like.

GLACE AU CITRON ET AU BASILIC
Lemon and Basil Ice Cream
6 Servings

The texture of this ice cream is silken and there is no mistaking the flavors. Make this in summer when the basil is fragrant and abundant. In winter you could replace the basil with 12 dried verbena leaves. Very French and very delicious.

1½ cups whole milk	¾ cup granulated sugar
2 cups loosely packed fresh basil leaves	4 egg yolks
Lemon peel from one lemon all white pith removed	The juice of one lemon
	¾ cup heavy cream

In a small saucepan heat the milk just to the boiling point and remove from the heat. Add the basil leaves and the lemon peel. Cover the pan and leave to infuse for one hour.

In a bowl, beat the egg yolks with the sugar until thick and pale yellow. Strain the milk over the egg mixture, pressing on the basil and lemon to extract all of the flavor you can.

Return this mixture to the saucepan and heat over a gentle fire stirring with a wooden spoon until the mixture thickens slightly. Remove from the heat, pour into a bowl and cool completely. When cold, add the lemon juice and the heavy cream. Put the mixture into an ice cream maker and freeze.

SOUPE AUX PECHES DE VIGNE A L'IRANCY
Warm Vine Peach Soup with Irancy Wine
8 Servings

Peche de Vigne is a variety of red-fleshed, late-ripening, flavorful peach. Called such because it's sometimes grown among the vines, it also goes by the name *'peche sanguine'* or 'blood peach'. Not too sweet, with a slight bitter edge, it has a unique cooking quality. Used in a savory preparation, it makes a nice accompaniment to game birds, for example.

8 ripe firm blood peaches
4 tablespoons unsalted butter
½ cup granulated sugar
2 cinnamon sticks

I cup Irancy wine (or light Pinot Noir)
Fresh mint for garnish
I quart vanilla ice cream (optional)

Blanch the peaches in boiling water for 2 minutes; you will notice they have very fuzzy skin. Remove the skins and quarter the peaches. In a sauté pan melt 2 tablespoons of the butter and add the peach quarters; sprinkle with a little sugar and cook until lightly caramelized, 5 minutes or so. Remove to a plate and reserve. In the same pan melt the rest of the butter add the remaining sugar and the cinnamon stick. Deglaze the pan with the Irancy wine. Reduce by half; then return the peaches to the pan to heat through. Serve in a warm bowl with some cookies (like almond *tuiles*) and scoop of vanilla ice cream if you like.

> WINE
>
> Irancy is one of the prettiest wine villages you'll ever see. Situated up near Chablis, it also makes some formidable Pinot. In a region mostly given over to white wine, Irancy produces red Burgundy worthy of the name. There are not many producers, but a high percentage of them do good work, so it can be a reasonable bet, picked blindly off the wine shop shelf. We like Thierry Richoux, and have been buying wine from them for over 20 years.

PAIN D'ÉPICES
Burgundian Spice Bread
Makes one loaf

Mustard, cassis and 'pain d'épices' are the triumvirate of Dijon's culinary reputation. This spice bread, laced with honey, has origins going back to the early Middle Ages when Burgundy was an emerging mercantile power, intrigued by the spices of the Orient.

Choose a quality, runny honey (I like acacia). And let the cake mellow, wrapped tightly, for a day or two before eating.

²/₃ cup runny honey	I tablespoon vegetable oil
¹/₃ cup dark brown sugar	2 teaspoons baking powder
I tablespoon vegetable oil	½ teaspoon vanilla extract
½ cup heavy cream	½ teaspoon each of ground ginger,
½ cup milk	cinnamon, clove and nutmeg
2 cups all purpose flour	¼ teaspoon salt

A I-quart rectangular loaf pan lightly oiled.

Preheat the oven to 325°F.

In a small saucepan gently heat the honey, sugar, cream and milk until just tepid. Let cool.

Put all the ingredients in the bowl of a food processor and mix until smooth. Alternatively in a large bowl stir all the ingredients together with a wooden spoon or mix with a wire whisk until well blended. Pour the batter into the prepared loaf pan and bake for 30–35 minutes until golden brown.

Let the bread cool slightly, then turn out of the baking pan and let cool completely. Wrap tightly in plastic wrap and let the cake develop its flavor for at least a day or two before slicing and serving.

PAIN D'ÉPICES PERDU AUX POIRES
Spice Bread Pudding with Pear
6 Servings

A quick, simple dessert with autumnal flavors.

12 thin slices of spice bread
6 firm but ripe pears such as Conference or Comice
¼ pound unsalted butter softened
²/₃ cup light brown sugar

2½ cups of milk
3 eggs
¹/₃ cup heavy cream
4 tablespoons *Poire William* pear liqueur

Preheat the oven to 425°F.

Lightly butter a large oven gratin dish.

Use 2/3 of the softened butter to spread on one side of the bread slices only. Lay the buttered side down in the gratin dish to cover the bottom overlapping if necessary.

Peel the pears and quarter them. In a large sauté pan melt the remaining butter over medium heat. Add the pear quarters and cook until lightly browned. Sprinkle with a little more than half of the light brown sugar and let the pears caramelize.

Heat the milk. Beat the eggs with the remaining sugar and whisk in the hot milk. Beat in the cream and pour over the spice bread.

Top the bread with the pear quarters rounded sides down and drizzle over the *Poire William* if using. Bake for 30–35 minutes until the pears are caramelized. Serve warm.

GLACE DE PAIN D'ÉPICES AUX POIRES CARAMELISÉES
Spice Bread Ice Cream with Caramelized Pears
6 Servings

Macerating the spice bread in warm milk infuses this ice cream with great flavors of honey and anise. Also the caramelized crumbs that are added at the end of the churning give it an unexpected spicy crunch. In total, you will need 3 slices of *pain d'épices*.

For the candied spice bread crumbs:
1/3 cup crumbled *pain d'épices*
1/4 cup unsalted butter
1/2 cup granulated sugar

For the ice cream:
2 cups heavy cream
1 cup whole milk

1/2 cup honey (such as acacia)
2 slices pain d'epices

For the carmelized pears:
3 pears (I use Bosc or Anjou pears)
2 tablespoons unsalted butter
Juice of 1/2 lemon
1/2 cup granulated sugar
1/4 cup water

Make the candied spice crumbs: Melt the butter in a sauté pan. Add the sugar and the crumbled spice cake and sauté over low heat for 10 minutes, tossing occasionally, until slightly caramelized. Turn the crumbs onto a cutting board and let cool. Reserve.

In a large saucepan heat the heavy cream, milk and honey until simmering. Remove from the heat and crumble in the slices of spice bread. Stir well to mix, cover the pan and let sit for 1 hour. Strain the mixture through a fine sieve into a clean bowl and chill the mixture until completely cool. Pour the chilled cream into an ice cream maker. When nearly ready, add the reserved candied crumbs. Let the crumbs mix in thoroughly. Put the ice cream in the freezer until you are ready to serve.

Peel the pears and slice them in half. Core, and slice each half into 3 slices. In a sauté pan melt the butter. Add the pear slices and the lemon juice. Toss to coat well. Add the sugar and cook over a medium fire until caramelized. Add the water to deglaze the caramel a bit. Reserve the pears warm.

Serve the warm pears with the *pain d'épices* ice cream.

PARFAIT DE RHUBARBE À LA FRAISE
Rhubarb and Strawberry Parfait
6 Servings

A perfect early summer dessert.

For the Coconut Crunch:
¼ cup chilled unsalted butter
¼ cup soft brown sugar
⅓ cup all purpose flour
⅓ cup finely chopped coconut

For the parfaits:
3 cups sliced fresh rhubarb cut into 1 inch pieces
⅓ cup granulated sugar
¼ cup fresh orange juice
1 cup heavy cream chilled
2 cups fresh strawberries sliced

Preheat the oven to 375°F.

Start by making the crumble. Mix all four crumble ingredients and with your fingers blend together until it resembles coarse meal. Put onto a small non-stick baking tray or cake pan and set aside.

In a glass pie dish mix the rhubarb with the sugar and orange juice tossing to coat the pieces, cover with foil. Put both the rhubarb and the crumble mixture in the upper third of the preheated oven. Bake the crumble for 10 minutes or until lightly browned. Remove from the oven and let cool and then crumble coarsely. Uncover the rhubarb and continue cooking until the rhubarb is soft and syrupy. Remove and let cool.

You'll need six parfait glasses or decorative wine glasses. Chill the glasses on a tray in the refrigerator.

Puree the rhubarb in a processor and chill in a bowl. Meanwhile beat the cream to soft peaks. Fold the cream into the rhubarb.

Sprinkle 1/3 of the crumble into the bottom of the glasses. Top with 2 table-spoons of the rhubarb cream. Add some sliced strawberries and top again with the cream. Top with more berries and then the remaining crumble. Chill for at least 1 hour and up to 8 before serving.

The Buffet

TARTES SALÉES
TARTS

TARTE AU CANTAL A LA TOMATE
Cantal Cheese and Tomato Tart

TARTE AUX ECHALOTES ET A L'ÉPOISSES
Shallot, Leek and Epoisses Cheese Tart

TARTE AU FROMAGE DE CHEVRE FRAIS A L'OSEILLE
Sorrel and Fresh Goat's Cheese Tart

TARTE A L'OIGNON
Onion Tart

TARTE AU ROQUEFORT AUX POIREAUX ET AUX EPINARDS
Leek, Spinach and Roquefort Tart

TARTE AU SAUMON, AUX POIREAUX ET A LA TOMATE
Salmon, Leek and Tomato Tart

TARTE AU FROMAGE DE CHEVRE ET AUX GIROLLES
Goat's Cheese and Chanterelle Mushroom Tart

PATE BRISÉE
Savory Pie Crust

TARTE AU CANTAL A LA TOMATE
Cantal Cheese and Tomato Tart
Serves 8

Call it pizza if you must! It's become a standing joke among guests who ask me to prepare this tart on every Papillon tour they take. Believe me, I understand why; it is good.

Cantal is a fruity cow's milk cheese coming from the Auvergne region and *Laguiole* is considered the king of cantals. I have seen some wonderful cheese counters in the states so search it out. It really makes a difference in the flavor of the finished tart.

One important counsel with this tart is to salt the tomato slices at least ½ hour before assembling the tart. Otherwise they will exude too much juice and the crust will be soggy.

The tart can be assembled and baked on a solid rectangle baking sheet or in a round fluted tart pan with removable bottom.

½ pound of puff pastry	½ pound of *Cantal* cheese
8 medium-sized ripe tomatoes	Fine sea salt
3 tablespoons of olive oil	Freshly ground black pepper
2 tablespoons of Dijon or full-grain mustard	1 tablespoon of fresh thyme or 1 teaspoon of dried

Slice the tomatoes thinly and place in a shallow dish. Sprinkle with salt and pepper, drizzle with the olive oil and let marinate for 30 minutes.

Preheat the oven to 400°F.

Roll out the chilled puff pastry in the form of your baking sheet, crimping the edges to form a shallow lip. Prick the pastry with a fork and chill in the refrigerator for 10 minutes.

Slice the cheese thinly. Drain the tomatoes. Take the pastry out of the refrigerator and brush it lightly with the mustard. Place a layer of cheese on the mustard, top with a decorative layer of tomatoes and sprinkle over the thyme leaves.

Bake for 35–40 minutes until the cheese bubbles up through the tomatoes and the base looks well cooked when lifted with a knife. Let sit 10 minutes before cutting and serving.

TARTE AUX ECHALOTES ET A L'ÉPOISSES
Shallot, Leek and Epoisses Cheese Tart
8–10 Servings

People who live around the village of Epoisses will tell you unequivocally that there is no better cheese on earth than 'their' *Epoisses*. And we heartily agree. But its one weak point is that it does not travel well. *Epoisses* is a whole milk soft cheese that is washed with *marc de Bourgogne* as it ages to keep it from developing a skin. When it is ripe and ready, it is a real *delice*. But when it is a little too old, it can become ammoniated, and too strong.

More and more, we're seeing *Epoisses* in good condition far away from its native Burgundy. If you find it in your specialty market, (I have seen it in Whole Foods Supermarkets on the east coast) look for a moist, brandy colored skin. It should fill its box, and not have shrunk away from the sides. Avoid dark orange, slimy skin. And sniff it to be sure it doe not smell of ammonia. Other smells are ok, though … it can be pretty pungent.

I like to serve this tart with a mixed green salad with walnut vinaigrette.

One *Pâte Brisée* tart shell blind baked. (see recipe)

2 tablespoons unsalted butter
4 medium leeks, white and pale green parts only

4 shallots sliced thinly
$^1/_3$ cup red wine vinegar
$^2/_3$ cup red wine
Freshly ground black pepper
1 *Epoisses* cheese (250 gr)

Preheat the oven to 400°F.

Blind bake the *pâte brisée* tart shell.

Cut the leeks into 1-inch pieces. Soak them in a large bowl filled with cold water for a half an hour to remove any grit. Blanch the leeks in boiling salted water for 5 minutes. Refresh by plunging them into very cold water. Place on paper towel to drain.

Sweat the shallots in a small sauté pan with the unsalted butter. When soft, add the vinegar, let bubble for a minute or two then add the red wine. Reduce this to nearly syrup.

Layer the bottom of the blind-baked tart shell with the shallot syrup. Add the leek pieces and the cubed *Epoisses*, grind over some black pepper. Bake for 10 minutes until the Epoisses has melted. Serve the tart immediately.

TARTE AU FROMAGE DE CHEVRE FRAIS A L'OSEILLE
Sorrel and Fresh Goat's Cheese Tart
8–10 Servings

We live near the village of Epoisses where the Berthaut people make the true Epoisses, what we locals consider the best cheese on earth. What's more, the little factory shop where they sell the cheese locally has reciprocal arrangements with other great cheese makers around the country. This means that we have an ever-changing selection of *crème de la crème* cheeses just down the road. One of these is the little *crottin du Morvan*, goat cheeses in 2 inch wide by 2 inch tall disks, which, when they are fresh, are wonderful in cooking, either baked whole in the oven to top a fluffy salad, or here as an ingredient in a baked tart.

If you don't find sorrel leaves, you could substitute arugula; though it will give you a different taste. Sorrel is a tart, almost sour flavor, where arugula is spicy, almost hot.

One *Pate Brisée* tart shell, blind baked (see recipe)

3 cups fresh sorrel leaves, washed and sliced thinly
2 shallots minced
2 tablespoons unsalted butter
2 eggs

½ cup *crème fraîche* or heavy cream
½ cup milk
Fine sea salt
Freshly ground black pepper
Scraping of nutmeg
4 *crottin de chevre* of 6 ounces of fresh goat's cheese
4 slices thin slices of bacon smoked

Preheat the oven to 375°F.

Blind bake the *pâte brisée* tart shell.

Chisel the sorrel leaves. Melt the butter in a sauté pan; add the minced shallots, season with salt and let sweat for a minute or two. Add the chiseled sorrel and wilt to a creamy texture. Remove from the heat and let cool slightly.

Mix the eggs, *crème fraîche*, milk, salt, pepper and nutmeg in a bowl.

Put the sorrel mixture in the bottom of the partially baked tart shell. Crumble over the goat's cheese and pour over the egg mixture. Cut the bacon slices into one inch pieces and sprinkle over the mixture. Grind over a bit of black pepper and bake the tart in the oven for 25-30 minutes until puffed and golden. Serve warm.

TARTE A L'OIGNON
Onion Tart
10–12 Servings

This rich onion tart is simple and honest, for the true onion lover. Serve in small slices along side a mixed green salad.

One 10 inch *Pâte Brisée* Tart Shell, uncooked (see recipe)

6 medium yellow onions, sliced thinly
2 tablespoons unsalted butter

Fine sea salt
Freshly ground black pepper
Scraping of nutmeg
2 cups of *crème fraîche* or heavy cream
2 large egg yolks

Preheat the oven to 375°F.

In a saucepan with a lid melt the butter, add the onion slices, season with salt, cover and let cook for 20 minutes over a low heat, stirring from time to time. The onions will stew in their own liquid and then start to dry out. Do not let them color. When soft and fairly dry remove from the heat.

Stir in the *crème fraîche,* season with additional salt (if needed) pepper and nutmeg. Let cool slightly, ten minutes or so, and then stir in the egg yolks, incorporating them well. Pour this into your tart base and bake for 35–40 until golden. Serve warm or at room temperature.

TARTE AU ROQUEFORT AUX POIREAUX ET AUX EPINARDS
Leek, Spinach and Roquefort Tart
8–12 Servings

Roquefort is a ewe's milk blue cheese that is matured in limestone caves under the town of Roquefort in south-west France. It is a naturally salty, sometimes very salty, so taste a little before seasoning the tart mixture.

One *Pâte Brisée* tart shell, blind baked (see recipe)

For the filling:
2 tablespoons unsalted butter
3 thin leeks, white and pale green parts only, sliced thinly and washed
¼ pound fresh spinach leaves, de-stemmed, washed and chopped coarsely

1 cup crumbled Roquefort cheese
3 whole medium eggs
1 cup heavy cream or *crème fraîche*
1 cup milk
Grated nutmeg
Fine sea salt
Freshly ground black pepper

Preheat the oven to 350°F.

Blind bake the *pâte brisée* tart shell

Melt the butter in a large sauté pan. When foaming, add the leeks, let sweat for 5 minutes to soften and then add the spinach. Cook until the spinach wilts. Let cool. Put the crumbled Roquefort over the base of your partially cooked pastry shell. In a bowl whisk the eggs with the cream and milk, and season with a generous grating of nutmeg and black pepper. Stir in the leeks and spinach. Pour this mixture over the Roquefort. Bake for 25–30 minutes until puffed and golden.

TARTE AU SAUMON, AUX POIREAUX ET A LA TOMATE
Salmon, Leek and Tomato Tart
8–12 Servings

This tart recipe is based on a one from the 3-star Michelin chef, George Blanc. I sometimes use thinly sliced savoy cabbage in place of the leeks when making the tart. All the different parts of this tart can be put together ahead of time and the tart assembled when ready to eat. Put it into bake as you are calling everyone to the table. The salmon cooks on top of the leek mixture and the tomatoes are placed on top of the salmon to keep it moist and luscious.

One *Pâte Brisée* tart shell, blind baked (see recipe)

5 medium leeks
¾ pound salmon filet
2 tablespoons unsalted butter

1 cup heavy cream
1 whole egg
4 tomatoes sliced thinly
Fine sea salt
Freshly ground black pepper

Preheat the oven to 375°F.

Blind bake the *pâte brisée* tart shell

Remove the dark green from the leeks and slice the pale green and white parts thinly. Soak the slices in a large bowl of cold water for 20 minutes to remove any grit.

Slice the salmon filet into 8-10 slices approximately ¼ inch thick.

In a large work bowl, whisk the egg with the cream. Season with salt and pepper.

Lift the leek slices from the water and drain. Melt the butter in a large sauté pan with a lid. Add the leeks, toss in the butter, cover the pan and cook until the leeks are soft but not colored, about 10 minutes or so. Let cool slightly.

Mix the leeks with the cream mixture and pour into the blind-baked tart shell. Top with the salmon slices, season with salt and pepper and then arrange the tomato slices on top. Bake for 15 minutes until just set. Serve immediately.

TARTE AU FROMAGE DE CHEVRE ET AUX GIROLLES
Goat's Cheese and Chanterelle Mushroom Tart
8–10 Servings

The French are avid mushroom hunters. To this day, mushroom season brings a celebration to the countryside. Though, as you might expect, it's not necessarily a communal celebration: folks are protective of their favorite spots and secretive about their take. It says a lot about the depth of the mushrooming tradition that French pharmacists still are trained to recognize comestible mushrooms from the dangerous ones. All you have to do is take your haul down to the local *pharmacie*, and someone there will tell you what's good and what's not.

Here we have lovely little chanterelles, what the French call *girolles*. This simple goat's cheese tart let's you appreciate the delicacy of the mushroom.

½ pound puff pastry
1 pound fresh chanterelle mushrooms
2 tablespoons unsalted butter
2 shallots minced
A large handful of fresh sorrel leaves chiseled

1 cup fresh creamy goat's cheese (like 'Chavroux')
½ cup *crème fraîche* or heavy cream (optional)
Fine sea salt

You will need two baking trays of similar size.

Preheat oven to 400°F.

Roll out the chilled puff pastry into a rectangle that will fit on your baking tray. Prick with a fork. Top with a piece of parchment paper and weight the pastry with the other tray. Bake the pastry for 20 minutes. Remove the tray and paper.

In a sauté pan melt 1 tablespoon of butter over a high heat. Add the mushrooms, season with a bit of salt, and sauté until the mushrooms release their liquid. Strain them and reserve the mushrooms on a plate. Add the other tablespoon of butter to the pan and sauté the shallot over medium heat and add the sorrel. When the sorrel has wilted return the mushrooms to the pan and remove from the heat. Season with salt to taste.

If the goat's cheese is rather dry mix with the cream. If it is quite creamy and spreadable this may not be necessary. Spread this mixture over the pastry rectangle. Top with mushrooms and bake for another 10 minutes. Serve warm.

PATE BRISÉE
Savory Pie Crust
Makes 2 10-inch tart shell bases

I like to use 10-inch fluted tart pans with removable bottoms rather than traditional quiche dishes. The savory tarts in this section that use a *pate brisée* are blind baked (with the exception of the Onion Tart which bakes for 40 minutes and needs no pre-cooking). Since this recipe makes enough dough for 2 tart bases you can freeze half the dough for another time. Just defrost it slowly over night in the fridge before using.

2 cups unbleached all-purpose flour	3 egg yolks
1 stick of cold unsalted butter, cubed	4 tablespoons of cold water
Pinch of salt	

Combine the flour, butter and salt in the bowl of a food processor. Blend for 20 seconds until the butter is well incorporated. Stop the machine and add the egg yolks and water. Process again until the mixture just starts to form a ball. Dust the pastry lightly with flour, cover in wax paper and let rest in the refrigerator for a half hour or so.

Divide the dough in half (freezing one half for another time) and roll out on a floured work surface. Line your tart pan with the dough, prick with a fork and refrigerate for at least an hour. I find that this pastry does not need to be weighted with beans or rice. It shrinks ever so slightly though you should try and fold the excess pastry over around the rim and pinch this to form a slightly higher pastry collar than the tart rim.

Preheat the oven to 400°F. Bake the tart shell for 20 minutes or so without coloring.

SALADES
BUFFET SALADS

SALADE DE BETTERAVES ROUGES ET VERTES
Roasted Beet Salad with Beet Greens

SALADE DE COCOS AUX CREVETTES
White Bean and Shrimp Salad

SALADE DE POULET AUX POIREAUX ET ROQUEFORT
Chicken Breast and Leek Salad with Roquefort Dressing

SALADE DE LENTILLES DU PUY AUX HERBES
Puy Lentil Salad with Shallots and Herbs

SALADE AIGRE-DOUCE DE CHOUX ROUGE AUX CERISES
Pickled Red Cabbage and Cherry Salad

SALADE DE FAUX FILET AUX ANCHOIS
Marinated Sirloin Beef Salad with Anchovy Dressing

SALADE DE CAROTTES CUITES A L'ORANGE ET AU CUMIN
Cooked Carrot Salad with Orange and Cumin

SALADE D'AVOCAT ET D'ENDIVES A LA MOUTARDE
Avocado and Belgian Endive Salad with a Mustard Sauce

SALADE DE POMMES DE TERRE RATTE AU CITRON ET A L'ANETH
Fingerling Potato, Lemon and Dill Salad

SALADE DE POIVRONS AU VINAIGRE DE XERES
Red Pepper Salad with Sherry Vinegar Glaze

SALADE DE COUSCOUS VERT
Green Couscous Salad

SALADE DE FRUITS DE MER
Mixed Seafood Salad

HARICOTS VERTS AUX ECHALOTES ET A LA CACAHOUETE
Green Bean Salad with Shallots and Peanuts

SALADE DE RIZ BASMATI AUX LEGUMES
Basmati Rice and Vegetable Salad

MELON DE CAVAILLON A LA VINAIGRETTE D'ANETH
Cavaillon Melon with Dill Vinaigrette

SALADE D'ORGE PERLÉ AU CITRON CONFIT
Pearl Barley Salad with Pickled Lemon

SALADE DE POIVRON ROUGE A L'HARISSA ET AU CITRON CONFIT
Red Pepper Salad with Harissa and Pickled Lemon

SALADE DE BETTERAVES ROUGES ET VERTES
Roasted Beet Salad with Beet Greens
6 Servings

Baking beets in the oven is the best way to concentrate their flavor and bring out their natural sweetness. They are a staple of our Burgundy garden, along with other root vegetables like turnips, carrots and Jerusalem artichokes. If you can buy them with the greens attached, so much the better; they are delicious.

12 small to medium beets with their greens attached
4 tablespoons extra virgin olive oil
3 cloves garlic, peeled and slightly smashed

2 tablespoons golden raisins
¼ cup pine nuts
½ teaspoon ground cumin

Preheat the oven to 375°F.

Twist off the beet tops and scrub the beets under water scrubbing them clean. Put them in a roasting dish and cover tightly with foil. Bake the beets for an hour or until tender when you test with a knife.

Strip the stalks off the beet greens and wash the tops in plenty of cold water to rid them of sand. Bring a medium saucepan to a boil with salted water. Blanch the greens for 2 minutes in boiling water then drain.

In a sauté pan with a cover, gently heat the olive oil with the garlic cloves, raisins and pine nuts. When the cloves start to turn golden add the beet greens. Season with salt, pepper and cumin. Cover the pan and cook for 5–10 minutes to blend the flavors. Remove from the heat, uncover and let cool.

When the beets are cool enough to handle, skin them and cut them into wedges. On a round serving plate make an outer circle of the beet wedges filling the inner circle with the greens. Season the wedges with sea salt, freshly ground black pepper and drizzle over some extra virgin olive oil. Serve at room temperature.

SALADE DE COCOS AUX CREVETTES
White Bean and Shrimp Salad
6–10 Servings

Fresh white 'coco' beans, still in their pods, make their appearance here on market stalls in mid-summer. With Tuscany being one of our favorite tour destinations, we have become true bean lovers. Burgundians may not quite have the choice of beans that the Tuscans do, but we do have 'cocos'! I've yet to find them in Italy, and you may not find them near you. But you can use fresh cranberry or cannellini beans in place of the 'cocos'. A handy tip: when they are in season you can shell them, bag them and freeze them for use in winter soups.

You can also serve this salad as a warm dish topped with either grilled fish or spicy chorizo sausages.

2 pounds fresh beans in the pod
Zest of two lemons
Juice of one lemon
¼ cup dry white wine
Fine sea salt
Freshly ground black pepper

1 pound small fresh boiled shrimp, peeled and de-veined

For the *crudo* salad:
2 celery stalks finely diced
1 red onion minced
3 cloves garlic minced
1 pound ripe red tomatoes, diced
Large handful flat leafed parsley coarsely chopped
Fine sea salt
Freshly ground black pepper
½ cup extra virgin olive oil

Mix all of the *crudo* ingredients except the olive together in a large bowl. Season with salt and pepper and make the *crudo* enough in advance so the vegetables have time to macerate while the beans are cooking.

Put the beans in a large pot, cover with cold water and bring to a boil. Simmer the beans for 30–40 minutes until just tender. Add 1 teaspoon of salt during the last 5 minutes of cooking, then drain the beans and put in a serving bowl. While the beans are hot, pour over the white wine, lemon zest and juice and season. Let cool gently tossing from time, being careful not to break up the beans.

Drain any juice that may have accumulated from the diced vegetables and season them with the olive oil. Add the *crudo* and shrimp to the bean salad toss gently and serve at room temperature. You could refrigerate covered overnight; but let the salad come to room temperature before serving.

SALADE DE POULET AUX POIREAUX ET ROQUEFORT
Chicken Breast and Leek Salad with Roquefort Dressing
6–8 Servings

Both Roquefort and leeks are naturally salty, so be careful when you season this salad. I've found this method for cooking chicken breast to be the best way to keep them moist for a salad; much better than poaching.

I sometimes sprinkle over toasted walnuts or pine nuts for a bit of added texture.

6 plump skinless free range chicken breasts
8 slender leeks
1 tablespoon of unsalted butter

For the dressing:
1 whole egg
1 teaspoon of white wine vinegar or the juice of ½ lemon

1 heaping teaspoon of Dijon mustard
1½ cups of light salad oil (such as canola oil)
Fine sea salt
Freshly ground black pepper
Reserved juice from cooking the breasts
½ cup crumbled Roquefort cheese
2 tablespoons chopped fresh tarragon

In a large non-stick sauté pan, gently melt the butter. Add the chicken breasts and cook over the lowest heat for about 15 to 20 minutes, turning once. They are done when the thickest part of the breast is springy to the touch. Let them cool in the pan in their juices. Reserve the juice for thinning the dressing.

Trim the leeks, removing and discarding about 2/3 of the dark green stem. Slice the leeks diagonally into 1-inch pieces. Soak them in a large bowl of cold water for about a half an hour to rid them of sand. Bring a pot of water to a boil and blanch the leeks for 3 minutes. Drain and plunge them into cold water to refresh them. Drain and place on paper towels to pat out excess moisture.

Make the dressing: Put the whole egg into the container of a processor along with the vinegar, mustard, salt and pepper. Process 20 seconds, then add the oil in a steady stream until thickened and emulsified. Stop. Add the Roquefort, tarragon and the reserved chicken juice and process for another 20 seconds to thin the sauce. It should be fairly liquid. If it needs more thinning just add some water. Taste for seasoning, adding more Roquefort if you like a stronger flavor.

Thinly slice the cooled chicken breasts. On a large oval platter make a bed of the leeks down the center. Drizzle over half of the dressing. Arrange the slices of breast meat on top, drizzle over a bit more of the dressing and serve the rest of the dressing in a bowl on the side.

SALADE DE LENTILLES DU PUY AUX HERBES
Puy Lentil Salad with Shallots and Herbs
8–10 Servings

Puy lentils are worth looking for. Grown on volcanic soil in the Auvergne region of France, they are the only lentil with an *appellation d'origine controlée*, and are now readily available in the US. They cook beautifully, holding their shape and texture, and are delicious when tossed with vinaigrette while still warm, as in this recipe.

Here in Burgundy, by chance, this same variety of lentil is grown near to us in the village of Bussy Rabutin. They are organically produced, a top-quality product. And who else can say that they have their own local lentil producer?

½ pound Puy lentils
2 cloves garlic peeled
1 bouquet garni (bay leaf, thyme, and parsley sprigs tied together
Fine sea salt

For the vinaigrette:
3 shallots peeled and minced
7 tablespoons good quality sherry vinegar
1 teaspoon fine sea salt
Freshly ground black pepper
7 tablespoons canola or grape seed oil
½ cup of chopped fresh herbs such as chives, chervil, dill, and parsley

Rinse the lentils under cold water and put them in a small saucepan. Cover with cold water, bring to a boil and then drain immediately. Rinse again and put them back into the saucepan covered with cold water. Add the garlic and bouquet garni. Bring to a boil and then simmer the lentils for 20 minutes or so until just done. When the lentils are nearly done, add a good pinch of salt. Strain again, remove the garlic and the bouquet garni and put the lentils in a salad bowl.

Make the vinaigrette by putting the shallots, sherry vinegar and salt in a bowl. Dissolve the salt and whisk in the oil. Add the pepper and herbs and pour over the warm lentils. Let cool to room temperature and serve.

SALADE AIGRE-DOUCE DE CHOUX ROUGE AUX CERISES
Pickled Red Cabbage and Cherry Salad
8–10 Servings

This pickled cabbage is good all on its own, but when cherries are in season they make the salad even more interesting. I like to serve this on a summer buffet table with the chicken breast and Roquefort salad and the Puy lentil salad.

½ of a medium-sized head of
red cabbage
2 cups of fairly tart red cherries pitted

For the pickling mixture:
⅓ cup red wine vinegar
⅓ cup granulated sugar
⅓ cup dry sherry

For the vinaigrette:
2 small shallots finely chopped
2 tablespoons sherry, red wine or white wine vinegar
2 tablespoons chopped fresh dill or
1 tablespoon chopped fresh tarragon
6 tablespoons of light salad oil such as canola
Fine sea salt
Freshly ground black pepper

Cut the half head of red cabbage in half and remove the core. Slice thinly, or shred as you would for cole slaw. Place the cabbage in a bowl with the pitted cherries.

Put the sugar, vinegar and dry sherry in a saucepan and bring to a boil. When the sugar has dissolved, pour the hot mixture over the cabbage and cherries. Toss well and continue to toss from time to time until the mixture cools to room temperature (at least 2 hours).

Make the vinaigrette by whisking the salt, vinegar, shallots and black pepper together in a bowl. Whisk in the oil and add the dill or tarragon.

Drain the cool and wilted cabbage in a colander, shaking off any excess liquid. Return to the bowl and toss with the vinaigrette. Serve at room temperature or slightly chilled.

SALADE DE FAUX FILET AUX ANCHOIS
Marinated Sirloin Beef Salad with Anchovy Dressing
10 Servings

Marinating the beef ahead will allow the spices to impregnate and flavor the meat. Searing the meat over a hot fire or on a heavy preheated griddle is important to seal in the juices and caramelize the spices. Let the meat rest for 10 minutes before slicing it thinly against the grain.

For the anchovy sauce, I prefer to use salted anchovies, but you can also use anchovies packed in oil.

Serve the beef with the spicy roasted peppers in sherry glaze and the green couscous salad.

For the marinade:
2 pounds sirloin cut into1 inch thick steaks
2 tablespoons red wine vinegar
Juice of a lemon
1 teaspoon nutmeg
1 teaspoon cinnamon
3 garlic cloves crushed
Freshly ground black pepper

For the vinaigrette:
Freshly ground black pepper
8 salted anchovy filets, rinsed and de-boned
2 cloves garlic crushed
2 thick slices of day-old rustic bread, crust removed, dipped in water and squeezed dry
2 teaspoons Dijon mustard
1 small handful fresh mint leaves
1 large bunch picked fresh parsley leaves
A few sprigs fresh tarragon or dill
½ cup extra virgin olive oil

Put the steaks onto a large flat platter and rub the marinade ingredients all over the meat. Let the meat sit with the marinade for a half and hour. Rub the steaks with a bit of olive oil just before grilling. Make sure your fire or griddle is hot so the meat sears. Cook the steaks to medium rare. Remove from the heat and let the meat rest while you prepare the sauce.

Make the anchovy sauce by putting all the ingredients except the olive oil in a food processor. Process for 1 minute; then add the oil in a thin steady stream until well emulsified. Stop. Taste for seasoning and add more salt and pepper if necessary.

With a sharp knife, cut the steaks into thin slices and serve with the sauce on the side.

SALADE DE CAROTTES CUITES A L'ORANGE ET AU CUMIN
Cooked Carrot Salad with Orange and Cumin
10 Servings

This salad has a North African accent, especially if you toss it with fresh coriander before serving.

10 carrots
1 orange
1 clove garlic
1 teaspoon coarse sea salt

2 tablespoon extra virgin olive oil
1 teaspoon ground cumin
2 tablespoons coarsely coriander or flat leaf parsley

Wash and peel the carrots and put them into a saucepan with a pinch of sea salt. Squeeze over the juice from one half of the orange and cover well with cold water and bring to a boil. Cook the carrots until easily pierced with a knife. Drain carefully and let cool slightly.

Meanwhile make the dressings. In a salad bowl with a pestle crush the peeled garlic clove with a teaspoon of coarse salt. When pulpy add the oil and ground cumin and then the juice of the other half of the orange. Stir in the coriander or parsley.

Slice the carrots decoratively on the angle and toss with the dressing. Serve at room temperature.

SALADE D'AVOCAT ET D'ENDIVES A LA MOUTARDE
Avocado and Belgian Endive Salad with a Mustard Sauce
6 Servings

This is the traditional mustard vinaigrette, ubiquitous in Burgundy. I use it on some of my favorite salads: anything from hot goat's cheese on greens with croutons to warm chicken livers sautéed with shallots and tossed with *laitue* (like Boston Bibb lettuce). Try it also with a *salade paysanne* – smoked-bacon lardons and a poached egg.

The trick to this dressing is to slowly whisk the oil into the mustard as you would when making a mayonnaise, and then to thin the vinaigrette with water at the end. Salt is not needed in the dressing, as the mustard is already somewhat salty. But you can add sea salt, if you like, sprinkled over the salad before serving.

For the salad:
2 ripe Haas avocados
3 cups of washed mâche (lambs lettuce or corn salad)
3 heads Belgian endive, outer leaves removed
½ cup coarsely chopped toasted hazelnuts or almonds

Fresh tarragon leaves
Freshly ground black pepper

For the mustard vinaigrette:
2 tablespoons plain Dijon mustard (preferably Fallot or Maille brands)
1 teaspoon white wine vinegar
¼ cup of light salad oil (such as canola oil)
3 tablespoons water

To make the vinaigrette, whisk the vinegar and mustard together in a bowl. Slowly add the oil in a stream, whisking until the sauce thickens and is emulsified. Slowly whisk in the water to thin and stabilize the vinaigrette.

Split the avocados in half. Peel and slice the halves into fairly thick slices widthwise. Cut the endive into 1-inch pieces, popping out the hard inner core. On a large platter or serving plate put down the mâche as a bed. Add the endive and avocado and sprinkle over the nuts and fresh tarragon leaves. Season the salad with freshly ground black pepper, and drizzle over the vinaigrette.

SALADE DE POMMES DE TERRE RATTE AU CITRON ET A L'ANETH
Fingerling Potato, Lemon and Dill Salad
6 Servings

Ratte potatoes are quality, smallish, dense, waxy potatoes, perfect for salads. Make this one with fingerling *ratte* potatoes or very small Yukon Gold potatoes, leaving the skins on for extra flavor.

2 pounds small new potatoes	1 teaspoon of dry Coleman's mustard
Zest of 3 lemons	(or a tablespoon of Dijon mustard)
5 tablespoons lemon juice	5 tablespoons extra virgin olive oil
1 teaspoon fine sea salt	3 tablespoons chopped dill
Freshly ground black pepper	

Scrub the potatoes, cutting larger ones in two and leaving the smaller ones whole. Put them in a large saucepan, cover with cold water and add a good pinch of coarse salt. Bring to a boil and cook the potatoes until they are just done, 25–35 minutes.

Wash and zest the lemons. Make the dressing by dissolving the sea salt in lemon juice. Whisk in the mustard and add the oil in a stream. Add the lemon zest, dill and a good amount of freshly ground pepper.

Add the dressing to the warm drained potatoes and toss to coat well. Let cool to room temperature and serve.

SALADE DE POIVRONS AU VINAIGRE DE XERES
Red Pepper Salad with Sherry Vinegar Glaze
10 Servings

When sautéing the garlic at the beginning of this recipe, it's important that the slices go to golden but no further, or they will turn bitter. Have your sherry vinegar ready and deglaze the pan at just the right moment.

When we are in the Basque Country in southwest France, I often use their spicy fresh *espelette* peppers. Red Anaheim or red bell peppers can be substituted. I grill them right on the barbecue, on a heavy griddle or under the broiler until the skin is blistered and evenly blackened.

20 Anaheim red peppers, roasted and skinned
3 cloves of garlic sliced thinly
4 tablespoons olive oil

2 tablespoons good quality sherry vinegar
Fine sea salt
Freshly ground black pepper
2 tablespoons chopped fresh parsley

In a heavy cast iron skillet heat the olive oil and garlic slices over a low fire until the garlic is golden. Immediately deglaze with the sherry vinegar. Add the grilled and peeled peppers, season with salt and pepper and cook the peppers in the sherry glaze for 5 minutes or so. Remove to a platter, cool, taste for seasoning and sprinkle over the parsley. Drizzle over a bit of olive oil and serve the peppers at room temperature.

SALADE DE COUSCOUS VERT
Green Couscous Salad
10 Servings

The color is really spectacular in this couscous dish. And it also has loads of flavor thanks to the mixture of blanched and pureed herbs. Use all four of the greens if you can; you'll get more complexity. But if you are missing one, just replace it with parsley, it will still be delicious.

This couscous could also be served warm with grilled lamb or chicken. Just add the pureed greens at the same time that you add the couscous. Let sit in a covered pan for 10 minutes flaking once or twice with a fork, then season with salt, pepper and a few pats of butter. Flake again with a fork and serve while still warm.

2 cups medium couscous	I cup picked parsley
2 cups water	I cup of chervil
2 teaspoons salt	3 tablespoons extra virgin olive oil
I cup fresh spinach leaves	Fine sea salt
I cup picked watercress leaves	Freshly ground black pepper

In a saucepan with a lid bring the 2 cups of water to a boil with a teaspoon of salt. When boiling add the couscous, stir, remove from the heat, cover and let sit for 10 minutes until the couscous swells.

Wash all the greens. Bring another pan of water to a boil with a teaspoon of salt. Have ready a bowl of ice water. Blanch the greens for 5 minutes in the boiling salted water, drain and immediately put them in the ice water. Let cool completely and then puree them in a blender.

Put the couscous in a large salad bowl and flake with a fork. Add the blanched greens. Season the couscous with the olive oil, salt and black pepper to taste.

SALADE DE FRUITS DE MER
Mixed Seafood Salad
8–10 Servings

This salad is worth every minute spent on it. It was one of my favorites when we were cruising on the Papillon. I somehow managed (with a little extra help from a crew member in peeling shrimp, picking mussels etc.) to assemble a whole buffet with this as its centerpiece by one o'clock. The just-cooked seafood tossed in a light mustard vinaigrette was perfect for summer days when we were moored up under a shady tree, waiting for the lock keepers to come back from their 2 hour lunch break.

1½ pounds of bay scallops, tough band and muscles removed
3 pounds of mussels
1½ pounds of small shrimp
1 pound filet of salmon
1 lemon
3 tablespoons chopped fresh chervil or chive
Fine sea salt and freshly ground black pepper

A bay leaf
1½ cups dry white wine

For the vinaigrette:
1 rounded tablespoon Dijon mustard
1 teaspoon white wine vinegar
¼ cup of light salad oil such as canola oil
3 tablespoons water

Cooking the scallops and salmon:
In a shallow sauté pan put 1½ cups of wine, 1 cup of water, 1 bay leaf, a few black peppercorns and a pinch of sea salt. Bring to the boil. Let reduce for 10 minutes, then turn the heat to low. Slide the salmon filet into the simmering liquid and cook for 5 minutes until it is just barely done. Remove and let cool. Add the scallops to the liquid, turn off the heat and let them cook in the poaching liquid for 5 minutes. Remove and let cool.

Scrub the mussels, pull off their 'beards' (the hairy bits that hang out of the shell) and wash in several changes of water. Discard any which are broken and those which feel very heavy or very light or which do not close when they are tapped or dipped in cold water. Steam them open by putting them in a saucepan with a half cup of water. Put the lid on and bring to a boil. As soon as they open remove them from the heat, let cool and then pick them from their shells.

Either steam or boil the shrimp. Let them cool. Peel and de-vein.

When all of the seafood is at room temperature, combine the shrimp, scallops, and mussels in a large bowl. Flake the salmon and add it to the bowl. Squeeze over the lemon juice, season with salt and pepper. Toss very gently.

Make the vinaigrette: In a small bowl whisk the mustard with the vinegar. Slowly add the oil, whisking until emulsified. Whisk in a little water to thin the vinaigrette. Add the chopped herbs and then pour this over the seafood. Toss again very lightly.

This salad is best served at room temperature the day it is made. If you must refrigerate it, remove from the fridge an hour before serving.

HARICOTS VERTS AUX ECHALOTES ET A LA CACAHOUETE
Green Bean Salad with Shallots and Peanuts
8–10 Servings

Macerating the shallots in the olive oil in advance helps to soften their taste. Use good quality sherry vinegar as well as a top-notch extra virgin olive oil for this recipe.

1 pound of thin fresh green beans, topped and tailed
2 tomatoes peeled, seeded and diced
½ cup of unsalted roasted peanuts, coarsely chopped

For the vinaigrette:
3 tablespoons of extra virgin olive oil
3 small shallots sliced thinly
1 teaspoon fine sea salt
1 tablespoon of sherry vinegar
A small splash of soy sauce

Put the olive oil and shallots in a small bowl and let macerate for an hour. Meanwhile bring a large pot of salted water to a boil and cook the green beans for 5 minutes until just tender but still somewhat crunchy. Drain and refresh the beans immediately in very cold water to keep their color. Put the beans on some paper towel to get rid of any excess moisture.

In a large salad bowl dissolve the salt in the sherry vinegar. Add the soy sauce and stir in the olive oil and shallots. Add the green beans, tomatoes and peanuts and toss to mix. Serve at room temperature.

SALADE DE RIZ BASMATI AUX LEGUMES
Basmati Rice and Vegetable Salad
8–10 Servings

I love the taste of basmati rice at room temperature, and in this salad the dressing is so light and fresh that the rice shines through. This goes very well with seafood, and I often serve it with the mixed seafood salad and the chilled melon and dill salad that you will also find in this section.

12 ounces basmati rice rinsed	1 tablespoon sesame oil
1 red bell pepper finely diced	1 tablespoon canola or grape seed oil
1 red onion halved and sliced thinly	1 large bunch fresh coriander leaves picked
2 cups shelled fresh peas	Fine sea salt
Juice of 3 limes	Freshly ground black pepper

Bring a large pot of salted water to a boil. When boiling, add the rice, reduce the heat and cook until the rice is just tender. Drain. Rinse the rice with cool water to remove the starch and put it in a large salad bowl. Reserve.

Bring another pot of salted water to a boil. When boiling, blanch the red pepper and the red onion for I minute, remove with a strainer and refresh in a large bowl of ice water. Add the peas to the boiling water and cook for 5 minutes, strain and refresh in the cold water. Drain the vegetables and remove excess water by placing them on paper towel. Add the vegetables to the rice, squeeze over the lime juice, and add the oils and coriander. Toss and season the salad to taste with the sea salt and black pepper.

Serve the salad at room temperature. If you want to make the salad a day in advance, leave out the lime juice, oils and seasoning and add them to the salad just before serving.

MELON DE CAVAILLON A LA VINAIGRETTE D'ANETH
Cavaillon Melon with Dill Vinaigrette
10 Servings

Here in France I use the musky 'Charentais' or 'Cavaillon' melon. They are generally smaller than what you would call a cantaloupe, but similar in taste and color. Technically, these are the only 'true' cantaloupes; American 'canteloupes' are actually a type of muskmelon.

You could turn this into a main salad by adding freshly cooked shrimp or lobster meat, and maybe some diced cucumber, cherry tomatoes and a bit of crumbled feta cheese. A perfect summer lunch.

I large melon, just ripe	Freshly ground white pepper
I tablespoon raspberry or sherry vinegar	2 shallots thinly sliced
½ teaspoon fine sea salt	2 tablespoons of freshly chopped tarragon
3 tablespoons canola or grape seed oil	

Cut the melon in half, scoop out the seeds and slice into fairly thin slices. Remove the rind from each slice and cut into small bite sized pieces.

Dissolve the sea salt in the raspberry vinegar. Whisk in the oil, white pepper, sliced shallots and chopped tarragon. Toss with the melon and serve on some chilled salad greens.

SALADE D'ORGE PERLÉ AU CITRON CONFIT
Pearl Barley Salad with Pickled Lemon
10 Servings

Avallon is a true market town, drawing in people from the surrounding villages and countryside. Many of the vendors are locals from the Morvan, a national park preserve, selling just what they produce or grow themselves. One of the exceptions, though, is the guy who sells olives. Compared with all the rustic, home-grown stalls of local produce, his selection wafts exoticism. Spices, dried fruit, nuts and every type of olive you can imagine. It's a colorful display, and you get lots of free samples! He also sells the pickled lemons that I use in this pearl barley salad. Lots of freshly chopped coriander, a pinch of cinnamon and some ground allspice give this salad a real Moroccan flavor.

This salad makes a great combination with grilled steak.

4 ounces pearl barley
2 pickled lemons, soaked covered in water
for 1 hour to remove excess salt
1 medium red onion finely diced
1 large bunch fresh coriander chopped

For the vinaigrette:
2 small cloves garlic minced
2 tablespoons red wine vinegar
Fine sea salt
Freshly ground black pepper
8 tablespoons extra virgin olive oil
½ teaspoon ground allspice
¼ teaspoon ground cinnamon

Rinse the barley and add to a fairly large pot of boiling water. Cook the barley until just done about 35–40 minutes. Drain and rinse briefly, under cool water to remove some of its starch. Let cool.

Cut the lemons in quarters and remove most of the pith and flesh and discard. Cut the quarters into strips and then dice. Put the barley, lemons, red onion and coriander in a large salad bowl.

In a small bowl whisk all of the vinaigrette ingredients together and pour this over the barley. Mix well, season to taste for salt and pepper. Serve the salad at room temperature.

SALADE DE POIVRONS ROUGES A L'HARISSA ET AU CITRON CONFIT
Red Pepper Salad with Harissa and Pickled Lemon
10 Servings

Harissa, the spicy North African pepper paste, is easily found throughout France. Put these peppers on a grilled baguette with goat's cheese and you have a great sandwich.

Try this with the Beef and Anchovy salad, the Green Couscous salad and the Carrot with Cumin and Orange for a well-balanced colorful buffet.

6 large red or yellow bell peppers
2 teaspoons harissa
4 tablespoons extra virgin olive oil
½ pickled lemon rinsed, pulp removed and rind diced

Fine sea salt
Torn rocket leaves or coarsely chopped flat leafed parsley

Pre-heat the oven to 375°F.

Wash and split the peppers in half. Remove seeds and put in one layer onto a roasting tray. Season the peppers with salt and a drizzle of olive oil. Add one cup of water to the bottom of the pan and cover tightly with foil. Place the tray in the middle of the oven and cook for 40 minutes. Remove the foil and continue to cook the peppers for an additional 30 minutes until most of the liquid has evaporated. Remove from the oven and let cool. Peel the pepper halves. In a salad bowl mix the harissa with the olive oil, the lemon and a pinch of sea salt. Add the peppers and toss gently to coat the peppers with the dressing. Put the peppers and their juices on a platter and scatter over the rocket or parsley and serve at room temperature.

INDEX

3245867

Made in the USA